PAGE ONE *to* PAGE DONE

PAGE ONE *to* PAGE DONE

A STEP-BY-STEP PLAN
TO WRITE, PUBLISH, AND MARKET YOUR AMAZING BOOK

NIKA MAPLES

bel esprit books
Dallas | Fort Worth

Page One to Page Done: A Step-By-Step Plan to Write, Publish, and Market Your Amazing Book
Nika Maples

Copyright © 2023 Nika Maples

Published by Bel Esprit Books, LLC
PO Box 821801
North Richland Hills, TX 76182

All rights reserved. Printed in the United States of America. No part of this book may be reproduced, stored in a retrieval system, or transmitted in any form and by any means—electronic, mechanical, photocopy, recording, or any other—except in the case of brief quotations in reviews, without written permission of the author.

Scripture quotations marked (ESV) are taken from the English Standard Version®. Text Edition: 2016. Copyright © 2001 by Crossway, a publishing ministry of Good News Publishers. The ESV® text has been reproduced in cooperation with and by permission of Good News Publishers. Unauthorized reproduction of this publication is prohibited. All rights reserved.

Scripture quotations marked (NIV) are taken from THE HOLY BIBLE, NEW INTERNATIONAL VERSION®, NIV® Copyright © 1973, 1978, 1984, 2011 by Biblica, Inc.® Used by permission. All rights reserved worldwide.

Scripture quotations marked (NLT) are taken from the Holy Bible, New Living Translation. Copyright © 1996, 2004, 2007 by Tyndale House Foundation. Used by permission of Tyndale House Publishers, Inc., Carol Stream, Illinois 60188. All rights reserved.

Scripture quotations marked (MSG) are taken from The Message. Copyright © 1993, 1994, 1995, 1996, 2000, 2001, 2002. Used by permission of NavPress Publishing Group.

The Living Bible copyright © 1971 by Tyndale House Foundation. Used by permission of Tyndale House Publishers Inc., Carol Stream, Illinois 60188. All rights reserved. The Living Bible, TLB, and the The Living Bible logo are registered trademarks of Tyndale House Publishers.

Scripture quotations marked TPT are from The Passion Translation®. Copyright © 2017, 2018 by Passion & Fire Ministries, Inc. Used by permission. All rights reserved. ThePassionTranslation.com.

Unless otherwise noted, all scriptures are NIV.

Cover art: Lea Ann Slotkin

Cover and interior design: Bel Esprit Books, LLC

Author photo: self-portrait

ISBN: 978-1-7331734-7-6

First Edition: January 2023

TO

ANOINTED WRITERS

*You have been prepared and
positioned for such a time as this.*

CONTENTS

INTRODUCTION

Step One: Planning & Developing

CHAPTER 1– PARTNER WITH <u>YOUR</u> AUTHOR	1
CHAPTER 2– PREPARE YOUR PATH WITH TRUTH	9
CHAPTER 3– ORGANIZE YOUR WRITING TIME	15
CHAPTER 4– CAPTURE & CONTAIN YOUR IDEAS	23
CHAPTER 5– GET TO KNOW YOUR PERSON	29
CHAPTER 6– DESIGN YOUR PROCESS & PROMISE	37
CHAPTER 7– CRAFT YOUR TITLE & SUBTITLE	45

Step Two: Outlining & Writing

CHAPTER 8– LIST YOUR TABLE OF CONTENTS	57
CHAPTER 9– STRUCTURE YOUR CHAPTERS	65
CHAPTER 10– FORMAT YOUR MANUSCRIPT	75
CHAPTER 11– CHOOSE YOUR VOICE	83
CHAPTER 12– UNDERSTAND YOUR EXPECTATIONS	91
CHAPTER 13– WRITE YOUR MANUSCRIPT	97
CHAPTER 14– CREATE YOUR READER EXPERIENCE	105

Step Three: Revising & Editing

CHAPTER 15– READ YOUR MANUSCRIPT	117
CHAPTER 16– POLISH YOUR MANUSCRIPT	123
CHAPTER 17– OFFER YOUR MANUSCRIPT	133
CHAPTER 18– REVISIT YOUR MANUSCRIPT	141

Step Four: Publishing & Launching

CHAPTER 19– WRITE YOUR BOOK PROPOSAL	151
CHAPTER 20– WORK WITH YOUR LITERARY AGENT	159
CHAPTER 21– JOIN YOUR PUBLISHING TEAM	167
CHAPTER 22– EXPAND YOUR SELF-PUBLISHING	175

Step Four: Marketing & Selling

CHAPTER 23– LAUNCH YOUR BOOK	187
CHAPTER 24– FIND YOUR BRAND VOICE — by Anita Albert-Watson	193
CHAPTER 25– ENJOY YOUR SELLING PROCESS	203
CHAPTER 26– HELP YOUR MEDIA PARTNERS — by Michelle Rupp	213
CHAPTER 27– SERVE YOUR PEOPLE — by Myron Golden	221

EXCERPT FROM TWELVE CLEAN PAGES

INTRODUCTION

THIS IS THE BOOK I WISH I'd had when I was working so hard to become an author, years ago.

God had commissioned me to be a writer *and* to call out writers; that much I knew. But He never told me how to do it. He simply let me figure it out, and of course, I felt unfit for the assignment. The insecurity and the invitation always arrive at the same time.

For me, the insecurity I felt about becoming an author came with the invitation to trust God in a new way. And as I call out the writer in you today, I guarantee you will receive the same opportunity.

Please, accept it.

I will help you. Within this book, I've given you every resource I could assemble in one place, including my philosophies and practices, biblical encouragement, writing exercises and activities in a downloadable workbook, templates, and instructional videos, as well as guest contributions from a few of my own coaches: Anita Albert-Watson, Michelle Rupp, and Myron Golden. I thought they could say some things better than I could. I hope you agree.

As you prepare to turn the page, stop and take a breath. You will never be the same after reading this book. Pause to thank God that He has brought you this far. He is about to take you even further. Fair warning, you will encounter doubt in the days ahead, and, at times, you will feel quite uncomfortable.

Doubt just means you are entering new territory.
And discomfort is the price of admission.

Download your workbook at
www.nikamaples.com/popd_workbook

STEP ONE

Planning & Developing

*Good planning and hard work lead to prosperity,
but hasty shortcuts lead to poverty.*

Proverbs 21:5 NLT

1

PARTNER WITH YOUR AUTHOR

IF I WERE AN ACTION HERO, I would want to be "Aunt Super Fun." I always look forward to the opportunity to babysit, dreaming up all kinds of outings, crafts, and games for my nieces and nephew, days in advance.

But sometimes things don't go according to plan.

On one memorable occasion, my brother and his wife took a weekend trip for their anniversary, leaving me to my favorite job. Everyone had an enjoyable first day, but it all changed when the three year-old woke up in the middle of the night, screaming. She had recently been through potty training and had never had an accident. But that night, she wet the bed and was crying because her "stomach" hurt. I changed the sheets and comforted her enough to help her fall asleep again.

An hour later, the same thing happened.

And in the early morning, it happened once more.

The bed-wetting and the level of pain she was experiencing told me that a urinary tract infection was the problem. As soon as the sun rose, I called her mother and told her about her daughter's three accidents, slight fever, and ongoing discomfort. She agreed that it sounded like a UTI. We discussed my taking her to the doctor for an antibiotic prescription.

"I have a few leftover training diapers in the top drawer. You should probably put her in one of those when you leave," she said just before we hung up.

A few minutes later, I sat down next to my niece with fresh clothes and a training diaper in my hands, and she wrinkled her nose. "Why do you have that?" she asked. "I don't need diapers anymore."

"I know, I know. But remember the accidents you had last night? You didn't mean to do it, but those accidents happened because you are a little bit sick. We gotta go to the doctor so you can get better."

"I don't want to wear a diaper!" she cried, erupting in tears. "I am not a baby anymore! I wear real underwear now!"

I brought her onto my lap. "It is just for today," I said. "You can take it off when you get home. But I don't want you to have another accident. So let's put it on, just in case."

The idea of taking off the diaper later did not console this child. Who cares about taking it *off*? She didn't want to put it *on* in the first place. I rocked her in my arms as she cried and cried. I knew she didn't feel good physically, but the diaper-suggestion had added insult to injury.

I asked the Lord to help me think of a way to communicate effectively with her. As I held her, I mentally rehearsed the right words to offer, searching for some sentence to convince her that she needed to put on the diaper. Nothing was coming to my mind.

Help me, Jesus, I prayed.

Right then, my niece lifted her head from my shoulder and looked at me through tears. "Ok, I'll do it," she said.

Fearing I would miss the cooperative window, I lost no time, quickly helping her put on the training diaper, as well as the rest of her clothes. When she was dressed and ready, I could resist my curiosity no longer. "What made you change your mind? A minute ago, you were really upset about this. Then suddenly you agreed and put on the training diaper with no problem," I said.

The old tears were still damp on her face when she said, "Well, in my class at church, my teacher told us that Jesus loves us. She showed us a picture of Jesus on the cross. She told us He died for us because He loves us so much."

"That's true," I said.

"And just now, I thought of that picture my teacher showed us. I never noticed it before, but Jesus was wearing a diaper when He was on the cross."

I stifled a giggle.

"So I still don't want to wear this," she said. "But if Jesus can wear a diaper, I can, too."

Wrapping my arms around her, I laughed. Now, I was the one with tears in my eyes. I had asked God for the best words to help my niece understand, and He hadn't given them to me.

He had given them to *her*.

EVERY PRINTED PAGE IS AN OPPORTUNITY FOR A CONVERSATION BETWEEN THE WRITER, THE READER, AND THE LORD WE BOTH SERVE.

My niece's revelation is the perfect illustration of the writing process. When I sit down at my laptop to work on a writing project, I pray and ask God for the best words. Sometimes He gives them to me. Other times, He gives them directly to the person reading my book.

After decades in this mysterious and glorious career as a Christian author, I have learned that books are a dialogue. Every printed page is an opportunity for a conversation between the writer, the reader, and the Lord we both serve. It is humbling to admit that the writer is not always part of the conversation. Often enough, God and the reader have a heart-to-heart of their own.

And that's fine by me.

As if I were the waitstaff in an elegant restaurant, I just want my books to deliver a dish of something delicious while I quietly back away, allowing the guests to enjoy a delightful evening around the table. I love knowing that my readers will leave the page encouraged, well-nourished in the Word, and strengthened to face another day.

Writing is one of my Kingdom assignments here on earth, and—thankfully!—most days, I want to do it.

But, like my niece, I must fix my eyes on Jesus and do it anyway, even on the days I don't want to.

AS IT TURNS OUT, THE AUTHOR OF LIFE MIGHT WANT TO TEACH US A THING OR TWO ABOUT WRITING.

If you picked up this book in search of guidance, I assume you are okay with me being your tender-yet-tough-as-nails writing coach throughout these pages. I am ready to train and push you, therefore, I won't wait until it is polite to ask:

Why do you want to write a book?

Why would you want to do something so challenging?

Why invest so much time to study writing?

And why *now*?

When you could spend your time in any way, why are you choosing to spend it this way? Time is the only thing that's irreplaceable, so the gift of your time is no small thing.

My guess is that you sense the Lord has been nudging you. He keeps whispering about a book. You know it might be one of your Kingdom assignments here on earth, but you feel stuck. Maybe you can't figure out how to write the thing. Or maybe you have written your book, but you don't know the first step to publishing it. Or maybe you have published your book, but you don't feel comfortable marketing and selling it, and your income has flatlined.

No matter your reason, you are in the right place. Come in; take a seat. I'll pour you a steaming cup of Earl Grey tea. Let's create the quiet and space to visit a while. I love helping Christian writers conquer what's holding them back so they can finish, publish, and market their amazing books. It is not easy, but it can be done while partnering with God. You and He can work together to create your **Kingdom-focused writing project**. He's equipped me to mentor you and show you how.

A Kingdom-focused writing project is what I call any book that is intentionally infused with biblical Truth, even if the content is not overtly centered on Christ. Christians often write books about business and lifestyle topics that are not obviously connected to the teachings of Jesus, yet they represent Him well. Both the Christ-centered book and the secular book can be Kingdom-focused when God calls the believer to write in alignment with Kingdom principles. Obedience to this call results in the special partnership I am talking about.

As it turns out, the Author of Life might want to teach us a thing or two about writing.

When we partner with God, it means that our Kingdom-focused writing projects no longer depend upon us because we follow His guidance, operate in His power, and trust His timing and results. It means we say yes to serving Him and no to our own willpower, fear, insecurity, and pride.

You see, something holy happens when a person submits their pen to the Lord. That kind of writer stops worrying so much and leans wholeheartedly into 1 Thessalonians 5:24: "The one who calls you is faithful, and He will do it" (NLT). This verse has proven true in my life, to be sure. I could never say that I created my writing career alone.

God did it in spite of me.

Like many authors, the magnetic pull to write a book started early for me, around seven or eight years old. I didn't know what I would write about, but I did writerly things—entering essay contests, becoming high school yearbook editor, filling notebooks with poetry, declaring journalism as my college major.

Then my sophomore year, life changed irrevocably when I experienced a massive brainstem stroke at age 20. It left me quadriplegic. For ten critical days, I was in the ICU, unable to speak or move or even blink. I could hardly breathe.

But I could hear.

On my third day of quadriplegia, I listened as a physician told my mother that I would likely have only 48 hours left to live, and if I did survive, I would remain in a vegetative state for the rest of my life.

For a moment, the room was silent. Then she spoke.

"How many people have recovered from a brain injury of this magnitude?" she asked. Even in my prison of paralysis, I could sense her steely resolve.

"Maybe …" the doctor hesitated before answering. "Maybe … *one*."

"One is all I need," she said.

If I could have smiled, I would have.

Bolstered by hope, I survived the 48-hour crisis window he predicted, and on the 10th day, they moved me from ICU to another part of the hospital where therapists would assess the abilities I might recover, if any. Expectations were low, to say the least. The major goal was lifting a spoon to my mouth. Walking wasn't even on the radar. But eventually I moved to a rehabilitation hospital, and a few months later, I had learned how to talk, feed myself, tie my shoes, and stand up between the parallel bars. Family and friends cheered as they watched me coming back to myself.

One day I told my therapist that I would never really be me unless I could do the thing I was born to do. And for that, I would need a typewriter. She made arrangements with the fourth floor nurses so that I could use a computer in the physical therapy gym after hours. Every night I wheeled myself straight from the cafeteria to the gym for writing time after dinner. It was an invigorating "workout" that always brought a smile to my face. My hands were spastic, but I was persistent. Day after day, I aimed my flailing arms, hoping they would strike the right keys. I made progress slowly, but before I was released from the rehabilitation hospital, I had written the entire first chapter of a book.

With just one finger.

At home, I gave up the impossible task of typing, and wrote the rest of my memoir with shaky cursive in ten composition notebooks. Then I gave the stack of notebooks to my aunt and asked her to type it all for me (hugs, Aunt Lisa!). My manuscript was finally in one digital file, and I had five copies printed and coil-bound at a copy shop. I kept two and sent the others directly to three Christian publishers.

I still have the rejection letters, which were thoughtful and kind.

Even so, I was devastated.

The manuscript I had sent them was my memoir, the story of a girl who had become quadriplegic due to a brainstem stroke and had defied the statistics to walk and talk again. Every sentence was drenched in the miraculous grace of God. If publishers had rejected *that* story, then I didn't know what kind of story they could possibly want. So I just stopped writing. My career as an author was over before it began. It never occurred to me to rewrite the manuscript or try again by sending it to other publishing houses.

I'd never even heard of a literary agent.

After reading that final rejection letter, every time I thought about my manuscript, I wanted to vomit. This may sound dramatic, but it will give you a window into my despair: I put one of the two remaining copies of the manuscript into a 55-gallon steel trash can and burned it. I put the last copy into the back of a filing cabinet drawer.

At only 21 years old, I felt defeated, convinced I wasn't meant to write a book. But like my very own Tell-Tale Heart, those words in the back of the drawer would not stay quiet.

I WOULD NEVER REALLY BE ME UNLESS I COULD DO THE ONE THING I WAS BORN TO DO. AND FOR THAT, I WOULD NEED A TYPEWRITER.

Fifteen years passed.

I became a high school English teacher, and every now and then, I would tell my students that I used to want to write a book. My girlhood dream was bloodied in the gutter, trying to drag itself out.

A few years later, I transferred from the high school and started teaching at an intermediate school. One day, I invited one of my former students, by then a college athlete, to visit my sixth grade class. I had asked him to share some inspiring words and sign a few footballs. At the end of that exciting afternoon, my twelve-year-old students reluctantly filed out the door, and RJ stayed a while to catch up with me. While I leaned on the corner of my desk, he half-spun back and forth in my chair and told me about his professors, coaches, and the new friends he had made at the university.

"What about you, huh? Whatever happened to that book you were going to write?"

"Oh, you remember that," I said, laughing it off.

"Of course I remember. So what happened to it?"

"It's … um … it's in a drawer," I stammered.

RJ stood up, a smile on his face. He stepped forward and said, "Ms. Maples, it's time to do what you were born to do."

For a moment, I couldn't breathe.

We wrapped it up and said our goodbyes, but I was still light-headed. His words had been a blow. I'd been forcefully reminded of the God who had created me for His delight. The Author of my life had written me into His story, calling me into a lifelong creative partnership with Him, but I had ignored the invitation.

That afternoon, I opened the filing cabinet drawer.

2

PREPARE YOUR PATH WITH TRUTH

THE VOLKSWAGEN BEETLE MADE OF PAPER caught my attention. It was easy to spot in the crowded parking lot because it was covered—bumper-to-bumper and tire-to-roof—in yellow sticky notes.

Almost magnetically, I made my way toward the paper car. The sticky notes appeared to be from an adoring beau. I got close enough to read a few of the messages:

You are the most beautiful woman in the world.
Every day, I thank God you are in my life.
There is nothing like the music of your laughter.
The world is better because you are in it.

Not wanting to intrude on a tender moment should the car owner return, I quickly went on my way. But I would have loved to have stayed to witness the joy this woman must have experienced when she came out to find her car had been "vandalized" in such a sweet way. Her husband or boyfriend may have been hiding nearby so that he could run to embrace her or help her collect all of the tiny notes. But even if he were not there, his beloved would have felt his presence because her car was covered by the adoring words he had left for her to find.

As I walked away, I couldn't help smiling. For a few seconds, I was lost in a daydream about what it would be like to see my own car, covered with love. After beholding that sight, it would be hard to get it out of your mind.

Yet, we forget that God has left all kinds of love notes, proving that He has gone before us. Somehow, that truth doesn't always stick.

The "Your Writing Journey" assignment I gave you in the downloadable workbook was intentional. It is good to remember the Lord's presence in your present and past.

But what about His presence in your future? Are you taking time to thank Him for that?

WE ARE GOD'S CO-CREATORS.
HE WANTS TO WORK ALONGSIDE US, NOT INSTEAD OF US.

Psalm 145:18 reminds us, "The Lord is near to those who call on Him." If you have asked God for help to write a book, then you are not alone in your Kingdom-focused writing project, even though it feels that way. The Holy Spirit is your willing partner. Sometimes you will sense His presence and sometimes you won't, but He will always, always, always be with you. So if you already know there will be some days when you won't feel God's presence (even though He is there) then why not prepare your path with the adoring words He has left for you?

If you take the time to do this, His words will be much more than just loving thoughts, written on sticky notes. They will become your **truth milestones**.

What is a milestone? The first definition in The Merriam-Webster Dictionary® is "a stone serving as a milepost." A milepost is set up beside a road to mark the distance in miles to a particular place. It tells how far you still have to go. If you have ever run a race, you know how important these are. Runners will keep going because they know they are headed in the right direction.

The second definition of milestone is "a significant point in development." That is an action or event marking a change in a person's life as they move forward in maturity. It tells how far you have come. Again, runners are profoundly encouraged to keep going when they see how far they have come.

You can count on both definitions of milestones to happen as you work on your Kingdom-focused writing project. You will move ahead in distance toward completion, and your soul will develop as you go. The Word of God is the perfect way to mark your journey. As you write, you need to be reminded that you can rely on it. Isaiah 40:8 proclaims that it "endures forever." See, I wasn't kidding when I said the Bible was a truth milestone. It is not going to move.

But you will.

Your truth milestones will mark how far you still have to go and how far you have come at the same time.

I'm leading you to do this at the beginning because I believe in the importance of God's supernatural partnership during your project. But many well-meaning Christian writers get it twisted by neglecting the *natural*, while focusing only on the *super*. We are God's co-creators. He wants to work alongside us, not instead of us.

So let's plan in the natural for a moment and get our fingernails dirty with a little work. Before you can create your truth milestones, you have to know your final destination and when you would like to arrive. Let's determine that now.

First, mark your **start date** on the calendar. If I were you, I would pick a week or two from today as your start date. You might want to read this entire book and complete the downloadable workbook before you start your official writing window.

In a later chapter, I will show you how to predict your specific **completion date**. Notice I prefer to call it your completion date instead of your *deadline*. This is purposeful because I believe our word choices have spiritual significance, something I will emphasize many times throughout this book. Why attach the word *dead* to any phase of your project when you don't have to?

If you haven't already noticed, words mean a lot to me.

For now, just trust me as your coach, and select an *estimated* completion date some time between three to six months from your start date. If you make your writing window much longer, you will use every moment of the time you have given yourself. It's just human nature.

The old adage known as Parkinson's Law says it well: Work expands to fill the time allotted for its completion.

As an illustration, apply this principle to the phenomenon of a woman's purse. When you temporarily switch from a small purse to a large one, the large one has plenty of empty space, right? At first it seems that a lot of the purse is left unused. But how long does that last? Eventually, you use all of the space you have. And conversely, if you typically carry a large purse and decide to switch to a smaller one, you will find that you are satisfied to bring only the essentials and have just enough room for them. At least for a little while.

No matter the size of your purse, it will always be full. And no matter the length of your writing window, you will always use all of it. So why not choose the smaller option?

When your start and completion dates are on the calendar, pause and play a song of worship. Rejoice and sing! This is no small thing. God helped you begin your writing momentum, and you took action with courage. You might even feel your heart beat faster when you see those dates actually on the calendar. That deserves a moment of acknowledgement.

Knowing your start date and completion date is engaging with the *natural* part of your supernatural partnership with God.

Now it is time to engage with the *super*.

Let me introduce you to a concept that I call **Holy Spirit highlighting**. There is nothing mystic or paranormal about this, so please do not confuse what I am about to explain with New Age ideas.

This is what Holy Spirit highlighting is to me:

Have you ever had a small message of encouragement stand out for you in an unusual or almost surreal way? Maybe it was a sentence you read or numbers you saw on a license plate or an image on a billboard. Maybe it was the lyrics in a song or a phrase someone said. Somehow it feels like the Holy Spirit has highlighted it for you, doesn't it? As you create Your truth milestones, I want you to pray for and expect Holy Spirit highlighting as you read the Bible. He will show you passages and verses that should be a focus for you as you write.

To create your unique truth milestones, you will need to spend some time thinking about your future self based on the Word of God. Who does He say you are? Who does He say you will be? The devil will try to tell you otherwise. So this list is how you will fight the battles of discouragement you may face in the days to come. You are going to consider one of your frequent setbacks or weaknesses, then ask the Holy Spirit for His highlighting, and lastly, do an Internet or concordance search for what the Bible says about the *opposite*. In this way, you will intentionally invite the Lord to turn your weaknesses into your strengths.

For instance, if you tend to struggle with insecurity, write "What does the Bible say about security" in a search engine.

When I did that, one of the first verses that came up was Psalm 16:8: "I have set the Lord always before me; because he is at my right hand, I shall not be shaken" (ESV). I like that one and want to use it as one of the truth milestones on my list of ten.

YOU CAN RELY ON THE BIBLE BECAUSE IT WON'T MOVE. EVERYTHING ELSE WILL.

Next, write that verse on a piece of paper beside number one, and then move on to line number two. (There is also a page in the downloadable workbook that you can use for this.) You can write multiple verses on the same topic or make all ten verses address different issues. When you have filled all ten spots, post your list in a prominent place and read it aloud every morning and every night.

My truth milestones are hanging on my refrigerator and sitting on my bedside table. I create a new list every three months, but you don't have to. In the time it takes for the coffee machine to brew one cup of coffee every morning, I turn around to the refrigerator and read my truth milestones out loud over my life and work. I do the same before I go to sleep at night.

There are days when it is easy to believe those statements. There are other days when it is not so easy. But I give voice to these verses anyway because they are truth, not because I feel them at the moment.

You may be tempted to use inspirational quotes or motivating phrases on your list, but the Bible is the only thing that can be a real milestone, showing you how far you have to go and how far you have come. You can rely on it because it won't move. Everything else will.

God's Word not only shows you where to go, but it changes you as you go.

Be aware that the change you desire will require something of you. We all want progress on our projects, but progress comes from producing, and producing comes from participating.

Don't expect God to spoon-feed you from the table He has prepared for you in the presence of your enemies (see Psalm 23:5). Participate. Get up and feed yourself. On those lonely or discouraging days of writing, when the urge to quit is heavy, you will want to stop producing. A day, a week, a month will go by without writing.

You can interrupt this pattern by walking over to your truth milestones and reading them out loud. Then doing it again. And again.

Participate.

Then get back to producing.

Progress is inevitable.

3

ORGANIZE YOUR WRITING TIME

SOME THINGS SHOULD NOT BE COMPARED. Nothing good comes from juxtaposing marriages, children, or friendships. These are evaluated qualitatively, and cannot be reduced to a number on a measuring stick or timeline. Look too closely at someone else's relationships, and your own may lose their shimmer. The same thing happens with the writing of books.

Even so, new writers want to know: "How long does it take to write a book?"

It is a reasonable question. We want to plan the next season of our lives; we want to get a bead on the future. But trouble comes when we look to the right and left instead of straight ahead. One glance at how fast the writer next to us is running their race, and we will trip and fall off the track.

In other words, there is no right answer for how long it takes to write a book. Everyone writes at their own pace. It takes as long as it takes.

Okay, okay. I won't go all "Yoda" on you, leaving you hanging with only the qualitative and immeasurable answer. More there is for you, young Jedi. If you are willing to do a little math with me, I'll show you the formula that I use to find a quantitative answer. There *is* a way to calculate and estimate the number of days it will take to write your book.

Before we begin, it is important to make the distinction between a book and a **manuscript**. You will often hear people say, "I'm writing a book," but that is a bit of a misnomer. What they are actually writing is a manuscript. A manuscript only becomes a book after it is published.

A helpful detail to know is that in the publishing industry, a single manuscript is abbreviated *ms* and multiple manuscripts are abbreviated *mss*. I already had a contract with my first literary agent before I learned that. He would email me about my "ms," and I wondered if I should let him know there was a typo. I had no clue what he meant.

Perhaps it will take a bit of pressure off to tell your friends and family that you are working on a manuscript, not a book.

Wait … *should* you tell your friends and family that you are writing a manuscript?

My recommendation is that if you choose to tell them, you should do it in a very limited way. This is because the simple act of talking about your manuscript extends the time it takes to write it.

You see, a writer in the process of writing a manuscript is a pressure cooker.

Maybe you are familiar with pressure cookers. They are large pots with lids that form an airtight seal, allowing steam to build inside the pot when the liquid starts to boil. The rising heat increases the pressure inside the pot. And the pressure forces the heat into the food, cooking it faster. You can turn a small valve to release the steam pressure when the food is ready.

In other words, if there is cooking left to be done, a cook has to keep the valve shut.

And if there is writing left to be done, a writer has to keep their mouth shut.

Our mouths are the small valves of our body that release all the pressure that has been building in our hearts. In many cases, keeping the valve shut is a bad thing. Just as a pressure cooker will explode if you try to remove the lid without first releasing the pressure, a person will explode with emotion if a circumstance "pulls off the lid" before the pressure has been released. We release the pressure in our hearts by opening our mouths and voicing our concerns through prayer, therapy, or authentic conversations.

Most definitely, there is a time and place to open our mouths and release the pressure. But in the case of a writer, I have come to believe it is better not to release the pressure of an unfinished manuscript.

I often think of the words of Jeremiah, the prolific writer and prophet in the Old Testament. In Jeremiah 20:9, he writes:

> But if I say I'll never mention the Lord
> or speak in his name,
> his word burns in my heart like a fire.
> It's like a fire in my bones!
> I am worn out trying to hold it in!
> I can't do it! (NLT)

Just like Jereimiah, a writer feels exhausted from trying to hold it in when the words start to burn like a fire inside. The rising heat increases the pressure within the heart. This is as it should be. The increasing pressure forces meaning and purpose into the words, and they start to cook. When the story or topic you want to write about really comes into focus, you may feel as though you are about to burst. Yes, the pressure needs somewhere to go, and the only release valve you need is a page.

All too often, you talk instead.

When friends ask, you are enthusiastic enough to explain the narrative, recite the points of the outline, and discuss the special features in detail. But then you sit down to write later, and you wonder where all the pressure has gone. The powerful motivation you felt this morning has dissipated like steam, and now you can't think of anything to write about this afternoon. This is one reason some writers take longer to finish.

So maintain the practice of sharing limited information with family and friends during the writing window.

People will inevitably ask, "What's your book about?"

Make your answer short and sweet. The only thing you need to tell them is Your Promise Bridge (Don't worry, we'll get to that in an upcoming chapter). And if they press you for more?

Well, I follow up by saying, "I can't wait for you to read it and find out!" It is a lighthearted approach, and it usually works well.

If you find joy in connecting and sharing your thoughts with others, I know it might be difficult for you to keep the valve closed.

You might be asking, "How long do I need to keep my manuscript and ideas under a tight seal?"

This brings us back to our original question: "How long does it take to write a manuscript?"

It is a simple equation that is unique to you. Ready to find out in six easy steps?

STEP ONE: NAME YOUR WORD COUNT GOAL

You need to have a **Word Count Goal** in mind, not a page goal. If you are writing a fiction book, the lowest mark to shoot for is about 90,000 words. But I'm guessing most of the writers reading this book are interested in writing nonfiction: memoirs, Christian lifestyle, inspirational, Bible study curriculum, devotionals, and so on. In that case, your word count is much lower.

In this book, I refer to my own books quite often. That is not because they are the best examples I could possibly use, it is because they are the examples about which I know the most! I don't know the word count of any other book on the market, but I sure know mine:

Twelve Clean Pages, my memoir, is about 75,000.

Everyday Genesis, a Christian lifestyle book, is 70,000.

Hunting Hope, another Christian lifestyle book, is about 50,000.

Keep Teaching and *Keep Going*, my daily devotional books, are about 30,000 each, which is interesting to me because they were a lot harder to write.

Let's pick a word count goal for you. If this is your first book, I would go with 50,000 as a rule of thumb. On a sheet of paper, write *Word Count Goal: 50,000 words*. (There is also a page in the downloadable workbook that you can use for this.) You can decide whatever number you want, but 50,000 is a safe bet. Right now, that might feel like a tremendous amount, but you would be surprised how fast it stacks up when you learn the system I am going to teach you.

STEP TWO: CHOOSE YOUR SESSION LENGTH

Skip a line underneath your word goal and write **Session Length**. Picture yourself sitting down for your typical writing session. When are you most likely to do it? Choose a block of time that is reasonable for you to have a writing session on a semi-regular basis. Don't visit the land of wishful thinking, here. We are looking for realism, not fantasy. Would you consistently be able to set aside 30 minutes? 60 minutes? If it would be nearly impossible for you to have two hours of uninterrupted time, don't aim for two hours. (Mom of a preschooler, I'm looking at you.)

Let's be honest. This is not your dream session I'm talking about. If your mind automatically went to a cabin in the woods or the sandy shade of a beachside bungalow when I asked you to picture yourself writing, then drop your imaginary plane ticket and come back to me. Like I said, you are unlikely to have two or three hours of uninterrupted time on a regular basis. But what about 25 minutes? Maybe not every day, but twice a week? Your session time is a small amount that you and your family can commit to. Write it next to the label, *Session Length*.

NO REAL POWER EVER COMES FROM YOUR WILL.

Some of my book coaching clients are surprised when I release them from their expectation that all "real writers" have a strict writing regimen. When someone tells me, "I don't have time to write," I assume they really mean to say, "A strict writing regimen does not fit my lifestyle."

Cool. Me, either.

Sure, some writers write in a regimented way, I've heard. But many don't. I only write when I have a strong and compelling idea for a potential book, and even then, not every day.

So if you are convinced you don't have time to write a book, I suggest making a decision about when it is sensible for you to write. There is no reason to make yourself write every morning before work or every night before you go to sleep or every weekend. If writing is a dream of your heart, then forcing yourself to do it will drain all the joy out of it and leave it feeling like a drudgery.

And you know what does the draining, right?

It's your willpower. Willpower is a terrible thing masquerading as something good. Willpower makes you think it is actually possible to maintain an impeccable streak of action every day. Then willpower punishes you when you can't keep the streak. It's both a mirage and a misery.

No real power ever comes from your will.

Read that again.

Where does real power come from, then?

The Bible tells us in Acts 1:8a that we "will receive **power** when the Holy Spirit comes upon [us]" (NLT, emphasis mine).

And 2 Timothy 1:7 we learn that "God has not given us a spirit of fear and timidity, but of **power**, love, and self-discipline" (NLT, emphasis mine).

And Ephesians 3:20 reminds us that all glory goes "to God, who is able, through his mighty **power** at work within us, to accomplish infinitely more than we might ask or think" (NLT, emphasis mine).

Power comes from the Holy Spirit. That means that perfect performance doesn't count anymore because it doesn't exist. So stop trying to have an unbroken streak and join me on Team No Streaks! It's a lot more fun to love yourself unconditionally, believe me. It means that when I do write a few days in a row, I am not more pleased with myself than when I don't write a few days in a row. I have made the beautiful decision to be pleased with myself based on one thing: whether I have faith.

Why did I choose faith as the evaluation mark? Because that is what pleases God about me. Hebrews 11:6 explains that "it is impossible to please God without faith. Anyone who wants to come to him must believe that God exists and that he rewards those who sincerely seek him" (NLT).

Sometimes the reward is a finished manuscript, written not by our own joy-draining willpower but with the pleasure of faith alone.

STEP THREE: FIND YOUR SESSION WORD COUNT

Skip a line underneath your session length and write **Session Word Count**. Before you go further with the formula, you will need to know how many words you can write in one writing session. In order to find that number, I am going to give you a nice and comfortable writing assignment in the downloadable workbook. Before you try that, I am going to show you how to apply the formula and make your calculations after you have your session word count.

Here's how: Right before you begin your writing assignment, you are going to set your timer for whatever you decided for your session length. You can write it out by hand in a journal, but it won't be easy to get a word count that way. I would use a computer, if I were you.

Do the writing assignment, and when the timer stops, then stop wherever you are, even if you haven't written your final sentence. Don't keep going. Like your high school English teacher used to say, "Pencils down!"

And what if the timer hasn't gone off, but you have already finished the assignment? Then don't stop! Keep writing until the timer goes off. Then you will have your session word count. Need to know how to find your word count? Plenty of YouTube videos will show you how to find your word count, depending on the software you are using.

STEP FOUR: DIVIDE YOUR WORD GOAL BY YOUR SESSION WORD COUNT

We'll finish the equation now. Skip a line underneath your session word count and write **Total Sessions**.

Let's say a writer named Kaycie can write 600 words in one writing session. I am going to write 600 beside *Session Word Count*. The equation is now getting somewhere. If Kaycie's word count goal is 50,000, and her session word count is 600, then it is going to take her about 83 sessions to write her book. She will write 83 beside the label, *Total Sessions*.

The question is, how many days or weeks is that?

STEP FIVE: ESTIMATE YOUR SESSIONS PER WEEK

Skip a line underneath your total sessions and write **Sessions Per Week**.

Kaycie thinks it is likely that she can have three sessions a week. She is going to write 3 beside the label, *Sessions Per Week*.

STEP SIX: DIVIDE YOUR TOTAL SESSIONS BY YOUR SESSIONS PER WEEK

Skip a line underneath your sessions per week and write **Estimated Completion Date**. Now, you will divide your total sessions by your sessions per week. The answer will be the number of weeks it will take to finish your manuscript.

For Kaycie, it is going to take about 27 weeks to write her manuscript. When Kaycie divides 27 by four, she discovers that it will take her between six to seven months to finish. She might go faster, and she might go slower, but at least she has an idea now. And after you finish your writing assignment in the downloadable workbook, so will you.

When you have an estimate of how long it might take to write your manuscript, don't hold it too tightly. It's only a general road map. Sometimes you will take a longer route; sometimes you will find a shortcut. No worries. You'll arrive in God's perfect timing.

Your real motivation to finish shouldn't be staying on track, it should be following Jesus. Then you'll never be behind schedule.

You'll be behind Him.

4

CAPTURE & CONTAIN YOUR IDEAS

A THIRTEEN-YEAR-OLD GIRL NAMED TERESA ABBOTT lives in my mind. Her father is a scientist, and one day she goes to his lab after school and discovers that he is heroically working to stop a disease that has the potential to destroy the human race. She keeps her knowledge a secret until her father dies suddenly, and when she finds the notes in his journal, she realizes that she is the only one who knows how to save the world.

Her story has been with me since I had the idea a few years ago.

Audrey King also lives in my mind. She's in her mid-thirties, and meets the love of her life at the same time she begins working as a nanny for a wealthy, demanding mother who controls every moment of Audrey's time. When Emmett finally tells her he is tired of being on the back burner and is moving to another state, Audrey has to choose between her love for her fiancé and her fear of leaving the children alone with the cruelty of their mother.

Her story has been with me a long time, too.

These are just two of the fiction stories I have been thinking about writing. There are more. And there are nonfiction ideas tossing around in my brain, too. Picture a front-loading dryer. My manuscript ideas are the clothes rumbling inside. Flashes of color spin around and around in the circular window.

But nothing will come of these ideas until I put them on paper.

It is a shame, isn't it? My guess is that when you read those two snippets, you wanted to know what happens to Teresa and Audrey. You wish I would tell you the rest of their stories, right? Unfortunately, I am the only one who knows how it all turns out, and that is unfair. Good book ideas are something to be shared, not kept to yourself.

Why?

Because good ideas are a gift from God, and a gift is not a gift until you give it to someone.

In the Sermon on the Mount, Jesus said it this way: "You are the light of the world. A town built on a hill cannot be hidden. Neither do people light a lamp and put it under a bowl. Instead they put it on its stand, and it gives light to everyone in the house. In the same way, let your light shine before others, that they may see your good deeds and glorify your Father in heaven" (Matthew 5:14-16).

Good ideas are luminous. They are refreshing. They are from God. He planned to transform mankind by dwelling inside us and sharing His good ideas, one at a time. It is by His life shining within that we make the whole world brighter. Hiding our ideas is like crawling into a corner with a bowl over our heads.

Would you consider for a moment that He designed you to shine? Your mind is sparkling with wonderful ideas like a Mason jar filled with lightning bugs. All you need to do is let them out.

Ready?

STEP ONE: LET OUT YOUR IDEAS

Grab a stack of sticky notes and a pen. Choose a topic to think about. Set a timer for 20 minutes. Write down everything you know about that topic. List everything you think someone else would want or need to know.

Thinking of a story or experience? Remembering a Bible verse or special quote from someone? Planning to share an insight or teach a lesson? Jot down a word or two on each sticky note, placing them on the wall nearest you.

I can hear you whispering to yourself. You're saying you can't think of a topic. This is nonsense. You can think of plenty of topics. But I will humor you and help you find a few to get started. Grab five sticky notes and answer this question: *What are your five favorite things in the whole world?*

Write one on each sticky note.

Chances are, the five things you just listed are five topics you could talk about all day long to anyone who would listen. Now pick one of them and finish this exercise, Steps 1-4. Then pick another one from the list of five favorite topics and repeat this exercise, Steps 1-4. Do it until one of the five favorite topics energizes you or until you think of another topic that does.

STEP TWO: GROUP YOUR IDEAS

When you have pulled out a lot of ideas from your brain, pouring them onto paper, you can stop and smile. That was an important step. Now set the timer again and arrange your ideas into rows or groups, putting similar items together. It is possible that you will experience clarity or breakthrough at this stage. Finally seeing all of your thoughts spread out in front of you is helpful. Maybe you will discover that you have more to write about than you thought. And maybe you will discover that you have a good start, but there are some gaps. Great news! Now that you see the gaps, you can go about filling them with research or intentional idea development.

STEP THREE: CONTAIN YOUR IDEAS

Now put everything from each group into a different "container." One of my best practices as a writer is creating containers for my ideas. These containers begin in the early stages of idea development and serve me all the way to the last page of my manuscript. Be aware, not everyone likes containing their ideas in the same ways.

THE STICKY NOTE SYSTEM: One of my favorite ways to contain my ideas is to use giant sticky notes, purchased from office supply stores. After looking over my groups from

Step 2, I pull off one giant sticky note per group of small sticky notes. Each giant sticky note is a container. I develop a working title to go at the top of the giant sticky note and label it with a marker. Then I place all of the small sticky notes in that group on the giant sticky note.

When I have placed all of the small sticky notes on giant (now labeled) sticky notes, I post them on the back of the pantry door or in the garage or laundry room. By now, you have probably figured out that this is going to become my manuscript outline. Each giant sticky note is a chapter. The items written on the small sticky notes are the things I plan to include in that chapter. I don't number the chapters because I want to be able to rearrange the order of the giant sticky notes later, if needed.

Here I should warn you that The Sticky Note System is the very one that taught me not everyone likes containing their ideas in the same ways. One time, I was working with a book coaching client, and I went to her house, armed with giant sticky notes. We labeled them, covered them with small sticky notes, and posted them all over her laundry room. There were two problems after that. First, her husband is orderly by nature, and sticky notes all over the walls bothered him. Second, they bothered her, too. Every time she went into that room to do laundry, the notes symbolized the writing she hadn't finished, and she felt terrible.

The next time I went to her house, all the sticky notes were gone.

THE LEGAL PAD SYSTEM: This is the system I use most often. I purchase a fresh legal pad and write the working book title and subtitle in the middle of the first page. Then I skip three pages and write the working title of the first chapter at the top of the page. I skip three pages, then write the working title of the second chapter at the top. On I go, skipping three pages between each chapter title. These containers can later be pulled out of the legal pad and rearranged in the best order.

I remember I used a pink legal pad for *Everyday Genesis* and a yellow legal pad for *Hunting Hope*. I can still see the butter-colored pages spread across my dining room table for days at a time, as I shifted and switched the chapter order into a progression that satisfied me.

THE DIRECT-TO-DOCUMENT SYSTEM: This means I make containers by using section breaks in Microsoft Word, Google Docs, or in the case of writing the manuscript for this book, by using folders in Scrivener. I rarely go direct-to-document because I am a kinesthetic learner, and seeing the big picture, as well as manipulating it, is how I think best. Please do not be fooled into believing that going direct-to-document means you will finish your manuscript faster just because you are already typing. Here's the truth: You will finish your manuscript faster when you have clarity of thought, no other reason. So if seeing your ideas like big puzzle pieces improves the coherence of your communication, then that is the way to go. There is no need to start typing before your message is ready in your mind.

STEP FOUR: FILL YOUR CONTAINERS

Now, you are ready to build your manuscript from the "inside out." Give yourself a period of time, perhaps two weeks, to fill your containers. This is your idea development period, and there is no pressure in this process. When you think of something you want to include in your manuscript, it needs to go into a container. For me, this looks like keeping a small pad of paper and a pen nearby—in my purse, on the kitchen window sill, by the bathroom mirror, and in the console of my car. Whenever an insight or memory strikes me, I jot it down. At the end of the day or at the end of the week, I take those notes and put them into the appropriate containers, either sticking them on the giant sticky note or writing them on the legal pad. The great thing about working this way is that later, I can move the smaller notes from one place to another. Please do not underestimate the power of letting your idea development last two weeks or a bit longer. Our minds tend to notice outside evidence to prove the thoughts we are already thinking.

Here is what I mean. One of my highest values is "uniqueness." I am not likely to purchase clothes along the lines of anything trending. If I have seen a particular style on a few people, I decide it is not unique enough, and I no longer like it as much. For instance, I like to buy a pair of shoes that I've never seen anyone wear before. But it never fails that as soon as I start wearing them regularly, I notice almost everyone has the same pair! I'm sure you've experienced the same thing, whether it be shoes, a purse, or a car. Those items did not show up out of thin air. They were probably there all along. But we paid attention to them after we had paid for our own. That's because we notice evidence of the thoughts we are already thinking.

That's bad news for the shoe lover who values uniqueness, perhaps, but great news for the writer. The moment you create containers, you have turned on the ignition of your intellect. It will silently hum in the background of everything you do until you finish the manuscript. Like a Google® web crawler, your brain will scan every interaction and circumstance you encounter, looking for proof of your theories. You will be sitting in church, and your pen will set your Bible page ablaze when the sermon sounds like the preacher has been reading your mind. Podcasts will speak to you; billboards will shout at you. You'll see your Siamese cat pawing at a grasshopper, and it will become the perfect illustration for the point you plan to make in Chapter 10.

Evidence will be everywhere.

Some of it is your beautiful brain at work. Some of it is your beautiful Master at work. Either way, the jewels you will find are the wild spoils of the writing life, and you must write them down on a sticky note or on a legal pad or on a napkin or on the back of your hand. Record a voice memo or make a new note in your phone, as fast as you can. Do something to capture and contain your ideas.

Don't presume you will remember the precious details when it is time to write.

All of it is vapor, and you will forget, my dear.

5

GET TO KNOW YOUR PERSON

WE INVITED EVERYONE TO MY BIRTHDAY PARTY. My whole first grade class and all the 7 year olds from Sunday school were coming. We held the bash in the church basement, and I wore a navy blue velvet dress with lace collar and cuffs. It was a look made complete by my having slept on pink sponge rollers the night before. This was 1981, and I looked like Nellie Oleson from *Little House on the Prairie*.

My mom had planned all kinds of party games and activities for the event, but the pièce de ré·sistance was a movie. These days, movies are the blasé babysitters at the end of every kid's birthday party, the place where little ones park until all the parents show up. But in the early 80s, video players weren't in every household. So it was uncommon to have a movie at a child's birthday party.

A real movie!

Well, actually, a *reel* movie.

My mother had borrowed a reel-to-reel projector and ordered *The Red Balloon* from a reel-to-reel movie rental shop. I was delighted when she told me about it. *The Red Balloon* was my favorite. I couldn't wait to share it with all my friends.

Before I go on, I must ask. Have you seen *The Red Balloon*?

No?

Oh, perhaps you know it by its original title, *Le Ballon Rouge*?

Again, no?

Well, it is a French film produced in 1956, and there is no need for subtitles because no one actually speaks in it. It is not, by definition, a silent film, but for all intents and purposes, it is a silent film. And this is the riveting plot: A little boy follows a red balloon around Paris.

That's pretty much it.

Back to my birthday party. For the first half hour, the church basement bustled. There was laughter, cake and too many presents to count. All of it was wonderful, but I was anticipating the movie surprise yet to come.

Finally, my mother summoned all the little children to gather 'round. My heart fluttered. She adjusted the projector to shine in a perfect rectangle of glory on a retractable screen. This was the moment my young poet's heart had been waiting for.

Sigh.

When the brief movie ended, I turned around to see how the other kids were reacting. That's when I discovered that no one was sitting near the projector but me. Every chair was empty. I'd been so spellbound, I hadn't noticed my friends had abandoned the movie to go play on the other side of the basement. At the time it hurt my feelings that they had all run off to have their own kind of fun. Now, I look back and laugh that we had shown a mostly-silent foreign film made in 1956 to a room full of first graders in 1981. Disney had not yet come of age, nor our attention spans reached the speed of Lightning McQueen, but even so.

Everyone did not love *The Red Balloon*.

The Red Balloon is not for everyone.

Please remember my first grade birthday party while embarking on your Kingdom-focused writing project. If I were to ask you who is going to read your book, would you say, "Everyone?"

Alas, I must pop your red balloon, dear writer.

Your book is not for everyone, but this is not bad news. Nor is it an uncommon mistake. I used to think my books were for everyone, too. It seems like a good thing to invite everyone to the party.

The opposite is true.

PEOPLE WILL NOT COME TO A PARTY THEY HAVE NOT BEEN INVITED TO.

In fact, here's another story about a party that will further illustrate my point. A few years ago, I had an idea to host a series of dinner parties, and I posted an invitation to my parties on Facebook for my friends to see. All were invited. My parties were for everyone.

So, guess how many people expressed interest?

Exactly zero.

Then I tried a different strategy. I sent sixteen handwritten invitations by snail mail. Can you guess how many people accepted, then? All of them but one.

There is an important lesson in that little story. People will not come to a party they have not been invited to. Unless an invitation goes to a specific address with a specific name on it, no one knows it is for them. When people see an "all-call," they usually think, "Is this really for me or for someone else?"

This is precisely what your ideal reader will be thinking when they see your book on a shelf or on a screen for the first time.

Do you know your ideal reader? You need to identify a specific person that you could send an invitation to. And by specific, I mean you need to know their gender, age (not a range), preferences, interests, setbacks, hang ups, dreams, favorite moments, and even their name. It feels risky to dial it in to that level, but you are not excluding people when you do this. You are only excluding people when you don't do it.

I learned this lesson the hard way.

When I started my podcast, I called it *The Keep Going Podcast,* and I wrote pleasant, Bible-based episodes for any Christian. I figured there were millions of podcast-listening Christians out there in the world. I didn't want to commit to one topic and exclude any of them. My podcast was for everyone. That means I would have a bigger audience, right?!

Cue the buzzer.

Two things happened as a result of my decision not to choose a niche. One, my show got lost in a sea of generic Christian content on podcast platforms. Two, I would draw a blank when I sat down to write and record so I didn't produce new episodes very often. What would I write about? Over the course of six years, I had a whopping portfolio of 58 episodes produced because I was broadcasting roughly nine episodes a year (face-palm). So you might say I didn't have as big of a listening audience as I'd hoped.

Then I decided to take my podcast seriously. I was late to my own party. I considered my options, prayed about it, listened to the Lord, and clearly sensed that the next step was to produce a podcast for a specific group of people: Christian women who wanted to write books.

And *The Keep Writing Podcast* was born.

It was time to try a different strategy. I had to send an invitation to a specific person. So I pictured a fictional Christian woman. Not a group of people, but one person: someone named Danielle. The more I thought about her, the more I was able to create her imaginary story.

Danielle is a 38 year-old mother of two boys—one sixteen, the other thirteen. She works as a high school counselor. She has taught a class at church for years and has always felt called to write a book. Her husband, Kevin, is supportive of her desire but sometimes gets weary of the way she talks about writing a book without really moving forward. From time to time, he gently asks if she has made any progress. She knows he means well, but when he says it, she senses she is being pushed, and it makes things worse.

Every once in a while, she gets up before the kids and sits down at her laptop on Saturday mornings with a hot cup of coffee in her hand and an instrumental playlist in her ears.

She is ready to write.

But nothing comes. She stares at the blank screen, deeply aware that she is not only disappointing herself, but also Kevin. He loves and believes in her, and she keeps telling herself that as soon as school is out for the summer she will finally buckle down and finish this silly book. Even as the thought crosses her mind, she laughs at herself. She has made that promise for the last five years. In fact, it's been a while since she enjoyed a vacation without thinking she should be spending her free time writing. A slow guilt has been seeping into every positive experience.

She is concerned that she might be exhausting her friends. Years ago, she would ask them to pray about her writing, but she doesn't anymore. It must sound foolish to them that she brings it up and then keeps doing nothing about it.

She follows other Christian writers like Priscilla Shirer and Emily P. Freeman on social media. She likes Priscilla's strength and Emily's softness. She can't decide if her own writing style is fire or fog, but she wishes she could write like they do. She often stops her scroll to check and see how many followers they have. Then she checks her own handful of followers and winces, putting down her phone.

Danielle's negative thought patterns cycle through the following points:

SHE SAYS:

I don't know how to find time to write.
I don't know what to do when I sit down to write.
I don't know which topic to choose.
I don't know which way to go with the topic I have chosen.
I don't know if what I'm writing is any good.
I don't know how to write like Priscilla or Emily (insert any admired author, here).
I don't know if anyone is going to want to read what I write.

SHE WONDERS:

Should I traditionally publish or self-publish?
How much does it cost to get a literary agent?
How big does my platform have to be?
How do I get a publishing deal?
Should I write the book proposal or the book first?
How long does my book have to be?
How do I get my book on Amazon and in Barnes & Noble?

SHE FEELS:
Confused
Overwhelmed
Frustrated
Afraid
Insecure
Unworthy
Underqualified

Then one day she stumbles upon The Keep Writing Podcast, *and from the moment she hears my voice, she knows she has found a kindred spirit.*

For the first time in a long time, she feels hope.

You may be wondering how I know all of these things about Danielle. Well, at first, I imagined her based on my memory of myself at the beginning of my writing career. These were the things I thought, wondered, and felt. But as time passed, I started reaching out through social media and via my email list to ask if anyone would be willing to have a 15-minute appointment with me on Zoom. I told them I wanted to ask them 25 simple questions just to get their honest feedback. I was surprised how many friends and strangers agreed.

These are the questions I asked them:

1. How did you hear about or find me?
2. How long have you been following my content?
3. Please rate my podcast on a scale of 1-10. Why do you feel this way?
4. Are you on Facebook or Instagram most often?
5. Have you ever watched a video of me on YouTube? Which one? What did you think?
6. Have you ever read one of my books? Which one? What did you think?
7. How long have you wanted to write a book?
8. What kind of book do you want to write?

9. How far are you in the writing process?
10. Have you ever been part of a writer's group or attended a writer's conference?
11. Have you ever tried to learn more about writing through books, courses, or videos?
12. Have you ever worked with a 1:1 mentor or writing coach?
13. What has been holding you back from finishing your book?
14. What do you want to know more about?
15. What is your biggest question about writing a book?
16. What is your biggest worry or fear about becoming an author?
17. What interests you most about the digital courses or the coaching program I offer?
18. Why is writing your book important right now?
19. What would having a published book be worth to you?
20. If you were living your dream life as a writer, what would it look like?
21. What bothers you most about the idea of never finishing your book?
22. Do you really want to feel better about this? Why?
23. What would it mean for your family if you finished your book?
24. What would it mean for your readers if you finished your book?
25. What would it mean for you if you finished your book?

This list of questions can be adapted to your area of expertise and the subject matter of your book. Please note that you have to be diligent to engage with your ideal reader when you conduct interviews, not just anyone. Your sister might be easy to talk to, but is she your ideal reader? Your ideal reader can be identified by the answer to this question: *Who stands to benefit the most from your book?*

When you invite the kind of person who stands to benefit the most into an interview, be vulnerable and honest and tell them that you are looking for sincere feedback in a 15-minute phone call or Zoom meeting. Most people are eager to share their opinions. But be sure to take a deep breath before they answer. Sometimes, it will be hard to hear what they think. After you have interviewed ten people, you will know the heart and mind of your ideal reader, and your manuscript will be easier to write. You'll stop making it generalized and start talking directly to your person. There are several pages in the downloadable workbook that will help you go deeper to imagine your ideal reader.

For now, let's go back to my ideal reader. Does my description of Danielle fit you, personally? If it does, then you know I have been intentionally inviting you to listen to my podcast, read my books, and watch my YouTube channel. I wrote this book for you. You are my ideal reader!

And if the description of Danielle doesn't fit you, then please know I was hoping you would come to the party, too. I'm so glad you are here. The fact that you came is proof that what I am saying works. It is a paradox, really. More people will come if you design your message for one person. All the beautiful people you aren't expecting will show up. Danielle will bring them with her. The more, the merrier.

So send a specific invitation. Then prepare the charcuterie tray and fill the vases with fresh flowers.

We won't even need to show a silent French film to know that your party is going to be très chic.

6

DESIGN YOUR PROCESS & PROMISE

STEPHEN SAW THE WORDS "HOPE HUNTER" in a dream. As soon as the sun rose over his hometown of Perth, Australia, he ran to his computer and searched for the words he had seen in his mind's eye, wondering if God were trying to tell him something.

When he hit enter, my face popped up.

Hunting Hope, my second book, had just been released, and my website, as well as all of my social media profiles read, "I am a hope hunter," under a headshot of me. It only took a few moments for Stephen to look deeper and discover the book. He ordered one.

In the time it took for a copy of *Hunting Hope* to reach his doorstep, the Lord had shown him someone who needed to read it. There was a woman in his small group who was going through a difficult time, and he was worried that she was so depressed she might lose the will to live.

Stephen didn't know it, but she was my ideal reader. I had written *Hunting Hope: Dig Through the Darkness to Find the Light* with her in mind. Every story, every lesson, every scripture, every analogy, every quotation—every word—was written for a woman who was walking through a season of heartache or bone-crushing trials and didn't want to go on.

Let that sink in.

There was a woman who couldn't bear to face another day … until she read my book. It begs the question: What if I hadn't written it?

The only reason I know Stephen's story about his friend is because he sent me a Facebook message to tell me that his friend's heart had been healed by God as she read my book, and she was improving every day.

At the close of his message, he wrote:

This woman/mother/wife has been changed — because of you.
Your story is spreading to the ends of the earth.

WE COLLECT THE DOTS.
GOD CONNECTS THE DOTS.

From where I sat in Fort Worth, Texas, those words were stunning. I had never imagined that my book would have an impact in Australia. I don't know why I had not considered how far my words could travel in the Internet age. I didn't have professional expertise to share as a therapist or theologian, only my personal experience with seasons of darkness. Needless to say, it profoundly humbled me to realize that the whole time I had been thinking about what to put in my book, God had been thinking about a woman halfway around the world and the exact moment she would need to read it.

This experience is what prompted a little phrase that my clients have heard me say countless times: *We collect the dots. God connects the dots.*

What I mean is that when we collect information and inspiration to fill our preferred container system for our book, we are collecting the "dots" that God will surely put to use in His way and in His time, connecting them in ways we cannot comprehend.

You are likely spending a lot of thought energy wondering what people will think of your book, and when you do, you are probably picturing the friends and family within 100 miles of your home, or at least within 100 likes of your social media profile. But the truth is, you have no clue who actually will read your book. Your words might save the life of someone on another continent, the friend of a friend you've never met, who simply Googled you because he had a dream.

You can't make this stuff up.

And you can't make it happen, either.

Only God knows the person who is waiting to read your book. The best you can do is imagine your ideal reader and write to her as if she is real.

Because, in my case, she was.

In the previous chapter, you got to know your person, and the next thing for you to do as an author is to give that ideal reader what they need. What your person needs is for you to design a process to help them get from where they are now to where they want to be, and then they need you to promise that the process works.

I know what's coming up for you, right now. You're thinking, "But how can I help my ideal reader? I am not an expert, pundit, celebrity, or scientist. Who am I to write this book?"

Remember, my book *Hunting Hope* had a massive impact in someone's life, even though I didn't have diplomas and certifications behind it. Friend, you don't have to have all of those things, either. You just have to be the person standing a few steps in front of your reader in line.

People say they don't like to stand in line, but they do. We like standing in line when the outcome is unknown. We like to observe what happens to the people just ahead of us. Then we can prepare ourselves for our turn.

I saw this principle when I went to the Texas Department of Motor Vehicles to renew my car's registration sticker. I took a number from the automated kiosk, and then sat down to wait and watch dozens of people walk to the counter to take care of various issues. As I listened for my number to be called, I could also overhear bits of conversation coming from the counter. I saw one woman renew her handicapped placard, and thought, *Oh, yes! I need to do that, too. Mine is out of date. I will make sure I ask for that after I get the registration.*

A few more people passed through the line, and I saw a woman being turned away because she had forgotten to bring a copy of her car insurance. I thought, *Noooo! That is the one thing I forgot! I have my driver's license, the state inspection documents, and the registration renewal notice, but I forgot my proof of insurance!*

Then I remembered I had a digital copy on my phone, and calmed down. I pulled it up quickly and was ready when my number was called. The registration took seconds, and I walked out with a renewed handicapped parking placard, as well.

When you study the people ahead of you in line, you have a better experience.

In fact, sometimes, it is nice to ask questions of the person who is only a few steps ahead of where we are, rather than the one a lot further down the road. The further you get, the more you forget.

You don't have to be an expert. The language and explanations of an expert might confuse your ideal reader. You just have to be ahead of them in line, and they will hang on every word you say. They want to get ready for the very next thing.

If you are wavering a bit about your ideal reader, please know that he or she can be different for each book that you write, for each podcast you record, and even for each speaking engagement you deliver.

YOU DON'T HAVE TO BE AN EXPERT. THE LANGUAGE AND EXPLANATIONS OF AN EXPERT MIGHT CONFUSE YOUR IDEAL READER.

Last year, I had three speaking engagements in the same month. I spoke for the administrators and teachers in a public school district convocation, for the faith-focused women in a Bible conference, and for the federal employees of the United States Nuclear Commission in a staff development training.

Needless to say, my ideal reader (listener) was different each time. So don't feel like you are making a lifetime commitment, here. It's not you and this one person until you both retire. But it does need to be just the two of you for the duration of the book. Then., perhaps, you will commit to a different reader for your next book. Be willing to focus on one person each time.

I have a friend who occasionally teaches women's classes and when she begins her lesson, she opens with, "I have been Divorced, have been Depressed, and have survived the Death of a loved one, so if you ever need help with one of The Three D's, I have plenty of personal experience, and I am here to serve you."

Now, that is a woman who knows her ideal reader, as well as the value of her life story. She's not trying to be an attorney, counselor, or doctor. But she knows a thing or two that those experts may not know because she has personal experience with divorce, depression, and death. She has the perspective of the reader she wants to serve. She is looking at the issue from the same side.

And so are you.

To help you find value in your personal experience, I have created two exercises: "Your Story Generator" and "Your Decade of Questions." Both can be found in the downloadable workbook. Notice how many amazing stories you've lived through. And notice the questions you used to have versus the wisdom you have now.

In addition to those exercises, it will motivate you to write down a few of "Your Heart Dates." A heart date is a date that is forever branded on your heart. It might be the day you married or had your first child. It might be the day you lost a loved one or had a traumatic experience. Now the juices are flowing, right? You've got a few heart dates. Think of the most important heart dates in your life, those that you always notice when the page of the calendar turns. Whether your countenance is glowing or gloomy when a heart date approaches, you know it will affect you every time. The rest of the world goes on like nothing is different from any other day, but *you* know something is different.

Oh, how well you know.

Want to learn one of my heart dates?

March 2, 1994.

That was the night I experienced the brainstem stroke I told you about in a previous chapter. I was only 20 years old.

Everything changed for me on that otherwise ordinary Wednesday. One minute, I was an enthusiastic college sophomore, who loved to eat pizza and hang out with friends. The next, I was in a vegetative state, being fed through a tube in my nose in the Intensive Care Unit.

It took months of rehabilitation before hope came into view. Now, I am better, but the road to recovery hasn't been circular, and it didn't bring me back around to the life I was living before. Things are different now.

Before March 2nd, I could walk easily.

After March 2nd, I cannot.

And, as you can imagine, there have been numerous doctors and professional experts involved in my story. I've seen neurologists, rheumatologists, cardiologists, nephrologists, psychologists, physical therapists, occupational therapists, speech therapists, and more. Yet none of them, not a single one of them, knows what it feels like to be in the Intensive Care Unit, unable to speak, swallow, blink, or do anything other than listen to your heart rate barely keeping the pace of 12 bpm on the monitor beside you.

The professional experts cannot meet my reader there.

But I can.

And on the day that a person is shaken to the core and crying out to the Lord with every desperate breath in their lungs, believe me, they are not going to run to someone in a white coat for comfort and understanding.

They are going to come to me.

And they are going to come to you.

So what will we offer in that moment?

We will offer a **process**.

If the word process sounds too clinical to you, then maybe you would prefer to think of it as directions on a road map. You are going to show your reader how to get to a better place.

Now, close your eyes. Think of where your reader is right now. Picture a YOU ARE HERE sign above their head. Now, picture yourself where you are now. You are far away from your reader, on the other side of a canyon with no bridge in between. Picture a YOU CAN BE HERE sign above your head. Now, imagine that your reader is calling out to you with hands cupped around their mouth, shouting, "How do I get over there? Can you show me the way?"

You won't shout your answer back to them. You will simply point to the process in your book. The steps of your process are the planks of a bridge you will build for them. By the time your person tries every step of your process, they will be on the other side with you.

This is the part when you snap out of the vision, open your eyes, turn to me and say, "Wait, wait, wait, Nika. I don't want to write one of those kinds of books. I just want to tell my story."

I know you do. Truly, I know you do because I did, too.

But the world has changed since the 1800s when a lovely story was valuable simply because it was lovely. Now people expect more. We are even way past the 1970s, when people liked an inspiring story simply because it was inspiring. And we're even past the 1990s, when people liked a motivating story simply because it was motivating.

In the post-millennial age, people still like stories, but they *want* results.

So your story will be valuable to your reader if it can produce results in their life. There is nothing inherently wrong or selfish about this. It is just the way we are now. Don't fight it, or you'll have a garage full of books that you have unintentionally fought to keep all to yourself.

Designing your process is not hard. You can do this, if you don't overthink it.

Imagine that there are three to seven planks in the hanging bridge from where your reader is to where you are. The number of planks can be flexible. But in general, try to keep it between three to seven. Less than three won't seem substantial to your reader. (Would you step out onto a hanging bridge with only two planks?) And more than seven will seem too long. The longer the bridge, the more frightening it looks. Your reader wants to get over that bridge as quickly as possible. They want to be able to see the other side before they start.

They will be able to see the end result if you give your bridge a name. That name is your book's promise. Once it is officially given a name, your process has become **The Promise**

Bridge, and it is really the only reason anyone buys a book, unless they are three hours into a flight cancellation on a stormy night at Dallas-Fort Worth Airport. Then they might buy whatever book is available at a kiosk and never think about the results it will create for them. But these people are also desperately trying to make dinner out of soda, chips, and candy bars so don't count their vote.

Use the diagram in the downloadable workbook to help you get a clear understanding of your reader's process and your book's promise.

What is the very first step that a reader would have to take? And then what is the logical next step, and the next logical step, and the next, until they get to where you are? I have provided several examples to help you get started.

As you do this foundational work, think of the key phases that the Lord has already brought you through. Even if you know you have further to go, look back and help your reader make progress over the ground where you have been.

As you do this important thought work, you might find it helpful to post 1 Peter 4:10 where you will see it often: "Each of you should use whatever gift you have received to serve others, as faithful stewards of God's grace in its various forms."

Keep reminding yourself that professional expertise is not required to serve others with your gifts.

But faithful stewardship is a must.

7

CRAFT YOUR TITLE & SUBTITLE

AS THE EVENT HOST INTRODUCED ME to the audience, I stood just off-stage, ready to walk up the steps to take the podium and microphone.

"And now, please put your hands together and help me welcome the author of *Twelve Blank Pages*, Nika Maples!"

I was already at the top of the steps by then and almost fell backward because I was laughing so hard. It was even challenging for me to walk across the stage because tears had filled my eyes. When I finally made it to the podium, I said, "Please buy my book after I speak today; I promise the pages won't be blank!"

Everybody laughed along with me.

The title of that book is *Twelve Clean Pages,* and I cannot tell you how many times people have botched it in my speaker introduction. My favorite was when someone introduced me as the author of *Twelve Ocean Pages.* Sounds like the sequel to *Titanic.*

I'm the only one to blame for these goofs. When I wrote my first book, the story of my diagnosis of systemic lupus and subsequent stroke recovery, I chose the title from a paragraph at the end of the second chapter:

> There were only twelve years before illness found me, only twelve pages left clean in my life. They represent the time before I opened this sketchbook heart to the

hand of a brilliant Artist— the Author and Perfecter of my faith. The pages turned since have been ruined gloriously.

On each day is an illustration of His grace.

After much prayer, I had decided to self-publish my memoir, and although I did a lot of research about best practices for printing and distribution, I did not give any thought to a subtitle. With such a vague and poetic title, that was a big mistake.

Twelve Clean Pages has sold well, but I know it would have sold much better if there had been a subtitle. I guess one of the greatest things about self-publishing is that I can go back and add one whenever I want to. Stay tuned.

May I help you by offering a bit of guidance that I never received?

Pay attention to your subtitle.

I like to tell my clients that an excellent book cover will make people stop their stroll … or stop their scroll.

An excellent title will make them walk over … or click over.

An excellent subtitle will make them pick up the book … or look up the book.

There's more, but I'll get to that in the next chapter.

For now, put a laser beam of your attention on creating an excellent subtitle, which should be a reflection of The Promise Bridge you made in the previous chapter, only with more detail. Your subtitle is even more important than your main title, so let go of it for now. Table that title. Set it aside. Don't spend any mental energy on it. Your title can be decided after your entire manuscript is finished.

But your subtitle cannot.

It comes before the writing.

To help you, I offer what I call "Your Subtitle Swipe File" in the downloadable workbook. I made it because I noticed some trends in popular subtitles. These are not all of the trends, of course, and many best-selling books do not follow these trends at all. However, Your Subtitle Swipe File is a terrific place to start, and it will help you gain traction in making your decision.

Before you begin playing with your own subtitle, stop and think again about your ideal reader. Are you already tired of thinking? I bet you never realized so much thought was necessary before the writing began. Lack of forethought is why most people do not finish the amazing book they dream of writing.

But that's not you. So far, you know where to find your ideal reader, you have thought of a name and characteristics and have invited them to read your book. And not only have you invited your ideal reader, you have considered genuine ways that your spiritual gifts intersect with their needs and wants, and how your personal experiences can provide a bridge for others to get where you are.

Do you realize that you have already done more, much more, than most authors ever do? I'm not kidding! Congratulations!

You are moving swiftly through the beginning stages of your book, and I am glad you are taking action on the plays I have called. A football coach's well-planned plays are only as good as the quarterback who's willing to run them, so you deserve some recognition. Everything you have completed so far is unseen by the reader, but God sees you. He and I both know this is challenging work. It is the hidden preparation that they will never know about. But it is also the part that, when it is left undone, leaves a reader feeling like something is missing in a book.

What is missing is *them*. The writer who didn't choose to spend time in forethought never clearly defined the reader or invited them. But the reader can't quite put their finger on why the book feels so empty. They lose interest and don't recommend it to their friends. The book never becomes a bestseller.

And the writer never knows what went wrong.

You won't have that experience because, hopefully, you have gained more clarity about the role of forethought in the writing of a book.

By now you have probably guessed that the text on the cover is your book's most valuable real estate. You won't be able to communicate a wordy promise to your reader. They want a promise that packs a punch in as few words as possible. Think of your subtitle as the tiny capsule on the cover of your book. It is a molecule, an atom, the smallest summary of your book that is possible. It isn't an afterthought to be added later. It is the driving idea throughout the manuscript. Subtitles don't belong in the last stage of your manuscript. They belong at the beginning stage, during idea development.

> **THINK OF YOUR SUBTITLE AS THE TINY CAPSULE ON THE COVER OF YOUR BOOK. IT IS A MOLECULE, AN ATOM, THE SMALLEST SUMMARY OF YOUR BOOK THAT IS POSSIBLE.**

When I wrote *Hunting Hope*, its original title and subtitle were *Winter: Surviving a Season of Darkness*. When my publisher insisted that we could not use the title *Winter*, I still was under the impression that I could keep my subtitle. I was comfortable with *Hunting Hope: Surviving a Season of Darkness*. My editor put a big no on that subtitle, too. When she explained why, I understood subtitles in a new way.

She said, "Subtitles are supposed to give readers a quick glimpse of themselves in a better way. Here, your promise sounds like the best they can hope for is to survive. Nobody wants to just survive. Give them something more compelling. How do they want to see themselves?"

Ok, I got it. That made sense. I started to think of my subtitle as a magic mirror. My ideal reader wants to look into it and see what is possible.

So my editor and I proceeded to have dozens of phone calls and emails about that pesky subtitle. I had piles and piles of scratch paper, on which I had scribbled countless versions. My editor would suggest something I didn't like. I would suggest something she didn't like.

Finally, I thought, *Hmm. My ideal reader is a woman named Paula in her forties who is quite depressed and feels as if she has had a huge blow because she recently found out some very bad news. Each day feels dark. She feels dark. So how does she wish she could see herself? What does she want more than anything?*

Light.

Bingo! But light wasn't a promise that I could deliver quickly or easily. A sweet and sappy promise of light would have come across as saccharine to someone in despair. So I wanted a subtitle that suggested a subtle shift that would require mental and emotional work. My final book title and subtitle became *Hunting Hope: Dig Through the Darkness to Find the Light.*

It makes sense that a lot of forethought is required if you want to give your spiritual gift in a classy way. People naturally recoil from writers who are braggadocious and loud about what they have to offer. That's how it comes across when there is too little thinking in advance. An ideal reader in need won't trust an author who comes across like a carnival barker.

But just because you don't shout about your process and promise doesn't mean you need to whisper, either. Don't make your ideal reader strain to hear you. You have a spiritual gift to give your reader, and in order for them to receive it, they have to know you are offering it.

Romans 11:29 tells us that "God's gifts and his call are irrevocable." That means the gifts inside you will never go away. They will burn and beg to be given until you finally find someone you are willing to offer them to. Take heart, your readers are going to love what they receive when they get inside your book. I bet they don't even know that they need it right now.

They are distracted by what they want, instead.

Your ideal reader may not know what he or she needs, but by the grace of God, you do. Take a good look at your ideal reader in your mind. They need something, don't they? What is it? And more importantly, what *want* is covering their *need*? As a simple example, the reader who wants more money might actually need a deeper connection with and more confidence in their Provider. And the reader who wants to stop people-pleasing behaviors, might actually need a new perspective on how to people-please in a way that blesses their own heart, too.

God may be sending you to your ideal reader to provide for needs that they don't even know they have. In 1 Peter 5:10, we are comforted that "the God of all grace, who called you to his eternal glory in Christ, after you have suffered a little while, will himself restore you and make you strong, firm and steadfast." God doesn't let His children stay in their problems forever, not when He can connect them to other children who will minister His grace at just the

right time. We all know what it feels like to receive the grace of another person's spiritual gift in our time of need. Life is a beautiful dance of giving and receiving. Through your published manuscript, the Lord is putting you in a purposed position to give exponentially.

God lets us know in Philippians 4:19 that He "will meet all [our] needs according to the riches of his glory in Christ Jesus." That goes for both you and your reader. God can meet their needs through you, and He can meet your needs through someone else. He might even be meeting your need to grow as a writer through me right now.

Yes, since we're on the subject, let's examine this little exchange right here. Look closely at you and me. Before I could help you, I had to figure out *how* I could help you. I had to picture what might be missing in your life and decide how I could meet your needs, even if you didn't know you had them. Where did I start? I prayed and asked the Lord for guidance, and I strongly felt that Him telling me that I could give you my spiritual gift, which is exhortation.

Exhortation is the encouragement to act.

I knew I could use my spiritual gift of exhortation to encourage you to act. My promise was simple, that my book would take you from the Land of No Book to the Land of Authorship. I named my promise The Keep Writing Bridge. In my mind, the only thing that would stop a reader from getting from The Land of No Book to the Land of Authorship would be if they quit writing. So I had to promise that I could exhort you to keep writing. Originally, I was thinking that *Keep Writing* would be a good title for this book. Later, it became obvious that *Page One to Page Done* was a better title, but it didn't matter because what had never changed was the subtitle. It remains the best summary of this book.

I knew you would need *A Step-by-Step Plan to Write, Publish, and Market Your Amazing Book* so that became my subtitle. (Truth be told, that is what you *want*. I know you *need* something else entirely, but that is mysteriously hidden throughout the pages of this book, and when the realization suddenly hits you, you will experience a flood of joy). Here's the beautiful secret: It is possible for an author to give a reader what they want and what they need at the same time.

The intersection of Want and Need is the point of connection where you and your reader meet. You already know that you invited them to read your book because you have tucked a gift inside the pages for them to find, but now you have to persuade them to accept the gift. That is your promise. It is your subtitle, and crafting it doesn't begin the way you expect.

Your subtitle begins with a great attitude.

Isn't it frustrating when you interact with the kind of person who acts differently every time you are around them? You never know whether you will be greeted with a smile or a furrowed brow. Your ideal reader wants to know exactly what to expect from you. Every time. You can't act certain one minute and unsure the next and expect them to keep turning pages and trusting you.

BEING AN AUTHOR GIVES YOU AUTHORITY.

Second Corinthians 9:7-8 exhorts us to "give what [we] have decided in [our] heart to give, not reluctantly or under compulsion, for God loves a cheerful giver. And God is able to bless [us] abundantly, so that in all things at all times, having all that [we] need, [we] will abound in every good work."

So be cheerful. God loves to see it. Put a big smile on your face. I mean, a *big* smile! Tell your ideal reader that you are going to give them what they want. Do it clearly. Don't hold back. Don't hesitate. You can present yourself as the authority on your book. It is not arrogant to do so. It is clear. Brene Brown says, "Clarity is kindness."

Being an author gives you authority. It gives you the authority to be confident and clear, to declare your promise and deliver your process. I know that feels awkward, at first. But it's no different than putting on a pair of brand new shoes. Eventually, you are going to have to put them on and walk through the discomfort if you are going to break them in.

The blisters won't get better if you leave the shoes in the closet.

Download your workbook at
www.nikamaples.com/popd_workbook

STEP TWO

Outlining & Writing

*All hard work brings a profit,
but mere talk leads only to poverty.*

Proverbs 14:3 NIV

8

LIST YOUR TABLE OF CONTENTS

MY NIECE WANTED CHOCOLATE, and she wanted it now. We had walked to a nearby park, played for a long time, and then walked all the way home again.

By then, she was tired. Really tired.

As she headed toward the living room to rest and look at some picture books, she happened to notice something on the kitchen counter. As if it were glowing like a treasure, a bottle of chocolate syrup caught her attention.

"Nika, will you pour that chocolate syrup straight into my mouth?"

"No. I know you are hungry, but you can't just eat empty sugar after playing so hard. You need to have some protein to renew your energy," I said, shaking my head. "We are about to have lunch."

"But please, please, please pour that chocolate syrup straight into my mouth!" Her tone of voice was insistent. She was the type of tired that makes an angelic five-year-old throw a fit over nothing, and there were already tears pooling in her widening eyes. I could see lava building inside the volcano. Suddenly, she had become obsessed over this idea of drinking straight chocolate syrup, and it was about to cause more hullabaloo than I had the heart for.

So I told her, "Ok, that's fine with me. I will pour chocolate syrup straight into your mouth ... for dessert. First you will need to choose whether you want a drumstick or thigh or wing for lunch!" I said. I had learned how to offer strategic choices as a form of behavior management back when I was a classroom teacher. But from the look on her face, my attempt to make chicken sound more exciting than chocolate had gotten a failing grade. I quickly moved the syrup bottle to the top of the refrigerator when she lunged for it.

Just then, the doorbell rang. Our lunch delivery was a perfectly-timed distraction.

A half hour later, we had finished our fried chicken with a side of friendly conversation, and I asked my niece to wipe her hands on her napkin while I walked over to the refrigerator to get a surprise. I came back with the syrup bottle and gushed, "Tah-dah!"

But no one was at the table.

She had completely forgotten about the chocolate syrup! I looked around the corner, and she was already flipping through some picture books on the living room floor.

I sighed and smiled. She thought she wanted sugar, but she'd been satisfied by protein.

Believe it or not, that story is a pretty good illustration of the point I'd like to make in this chapter. Sugar comes after protein. New authors tend to obsess over the sticky-sweet parts of their books: the clever writing, the data or illustrations, the title, the cover design, the publisher. Those things have the wow-factor that we think we need as writers. But they are as nutrient-empty as chocolate syrup.

The protein of your book is your process. Without that, your reader will not be satisfied, and neither will you. Your **Table of Contents** is where your reader experiences the first sensation of fullness that they are hungry for.

In a previous chapter, I told you that an excellent book cover will make people stop their stroll ... or stop their scroll.

An excellent title will make them walk over ... or click over.

An excellent subtitle will make them pick up the book ... or look up the book.

An excellent back cover will make them look inside the front cover ... or look inside the digital cover.

Then, once your reader opens the cover of your book, an excellent Table of Contents will make them buy it.

First Corinthians 14:40 reads, "Everything should be done in a fitting and orderly way." And verse 33 of the same chapter says, "God is not a God of disorder but of peace." All you have to do is look at nature to know that God created the earth in an organized way. I think He knew it would be satisfying to human souls to experience order all around us. Everything fits. From the layers of a pine cone to the petals of a daisy to the chambers of a nautilus.

When your reader takes a look at your Table of Contents (TOC) and sees the deliberate order in your process, it will feel satisfying to them. Order looks like planning and feels like peace. A clear TOC helps you trust the one who designed it. You want your reader to see the beauty of your plan and experience peace from cover to cover.

It is time for the process and The Promise Bridge you have crafted to be expanded into a TOC. But before I tell you how to do it, I'll let you in on a little secret: A Table of Contents is just an outline.

ONCE YOUR READER OPENS THE COVER OF YOUR BOOK, AN EXCELLENT TABLE OF CONTENTS WILL MAKE THEM BUY IT.

When I taught high school English, I would ask my students to turn in their research papers in stages. The first stage was a simple pre-writing paragraph—a basic pitch of the idea for their paper. Ideas come before anything else.

But after ideas is order, and when I asked my students to enter the second stage and turn in an outline—a logical process for how they would present their idea—there was considerable pushback. Many of them, and by that I actually mean *most* of them, asked if they could turn in their outlines *after* they turned in their rough drafts. They said it was faster and easier to write their outlines after they had written the paper itself.

Huh?

Didn't they know that writing the outline makes writing the rough draft faster and easier, not the other way around? I couldn't convince them that they were missing an opportunity to speed up their work and make it more enjoyable by developing their outline first. To them, it felt like busy work.

I can understand why adolescents don't embrace the beauty of an outline, but I have faced some of the same resistant conversations as a book coach who advises adult writers. Over the years, several of my clients have brushed off the suggestion to write a detailed outline, saying that they would write it *after* they finish the rough draft of their manuscript.

Huh?

Part of me thinks that there is a connection between the high school students I once taught and the clients I coach now. And that connection, I believe, is the English class itself. Hear me out. Almost all of us have been through an English class that had elements we did not appreciate or enjoy, including a wheelbarrow's worth of busy work. So outline-writing may have left a, shall we say, bad taste in our mouths.

It tastes like chicken when we wanted chocolate.

But outline-writing is not a meaningless assignment. If you write a detailed outline, it will eventually become your book's Table of Contents. Your reader is going to see this before they read another word you've written, so think of your outline as the first impression you can't repeat.

It's *that* important.

When I show you what a detailed, process-driven outline can do for you (the guide for your outline can be found in the downloadable workbook), you are going to be delighted. Decide right now that you love your outline! If you follow my advice to put your outline to work within your document instead of just setting it aside, never to be consulted again, then you will find writing your manuscript will be a pleasure.

So let's begin your outline by using the process you designed for your reader. As I said, that process can be thought of as the planks on The Promise Bridge. Those planks are the steps your reader has to take to get from where they are to where they want to be. Using this book as an example, the five steps of my process to take you from the Land of No Book to the Land of Authorship are:

STEP ONE: PLANNING & DEVELOPING
STEP TWO: OUTLINING & WRITING
STEP THREE: REVISING & EDITING
STEP FOUR: PUBLISHING & LAUNCHING
STEP FIVE: MARKETING & SELLING

Now take a moment to turn back and look closely at the TOC for this book. Notice how I have taken those steps—the planks in my Promise Bridge—and made them the main sections of the book. I called them steps, but it doesn't matter if you call them steps, sections, parts, or units, they will still be the main organizational tool for your message. When you were in your high school English class, your teacher tried to explain that these primary divisions were the Roman numerals of your outline. Is it all coming back now?

Getting this far is what I call a Level 1 Outline, and I've seen some new authors only make it to this point before they stop outlining and begin writing the manuscript. I believe they have a weaker book because of it. I recommend that you use the page in the downloadable workbook to document your Level 1 Outline.

Writers always say that they dread facing a blank page. Facing blank pages is just part of the experience of writing. You do have to face a blank page, but you don't have to be bullied by one. There is a way to take control of those pages and show them who's boss. And it all starts with that Level 1 Outline you just composed. Your outline may be slightly polished over the next few weeks, but most of it will not change because it is the backbone of your book. Not only is it the backbone, it's your book's best friend.

Next, take your outline to Level 2. Your Level 2 Outline is just questions, organized within the main sections. I have included my Level 2 Outline for *Page One to Page Done* in the downloadable workbook. There is also a page where you can write your own.

Focus on what your reader is wondering. What are the questions that they will be asking at every step of your process? Listing these will help you stay present at the precise location of your reader's journey and resist jumping ahead of yourself. You can't address your reader as if they are already at the final destination if they aren't even close, yet. You need to focus on providing the answers they seek right where they are.

Again using this book as an example, look at my Level 2 Outline in the downloadable workbook and notice the questions I expected you to be asking along the way. To create this list of questions, I didn't even have any chapters developed. I simply listed as many questions as I could under the five major sections that were part of my process.

This is the tedious planning that produces a fabulous book. Developing a Level 2 Outline that answers questions for your reader will keep the two of you connected. To discover the questions your reader is asking (or will be asking), refer to some of the notes you took during your interviews with ideal readers. Or think back to your own questions, the things that were constantly on your mind as you walked through this process for yourself. List as many questions as you can, all categorized within the steps of your process.

Finally, take your outline to Level 3. Your Level 3 Outline is the list of specific chapters you want to have in each primary division.

Look again at the TOC of this book and pay attention to how I took each primary division in my five-step process and broke it down into baby steps—the chapters. While your process itself should be three to seven steps, it doesn't matter how many chapters are in each section, as long as they are intentional.

My advice for you at the Level 3 stage of creating your outline is to think of your chapters in terms of a pattern. Remember, humans are satisfied by a sense of order and peace. So you can title your chapters with that in mind. Some authors do this by beginning the first word of every chapter title with the same letter. Some authors create a pattern by repeating the ends of words in their chapter titles, like "-tion" or "-ing" or "-ed." Some do it with rhyming chapter titles. I did it by beginning every chapter title with a verb and including the word "your" every time.

It bears repeating that there is an important reason for this. As you create your Level 1, 2, and 3 Outlines, you are actually listing your Table of Contents in magnificent detail. And if you think of the TOC as the first page of your manuscript, technically, you already have moved from planning to writing. Pen is on paper. Letters are being typed. The good and quiet work of authorship has begun.

But as your coach, I feel I must warn you that from this point forward, there will be two voices battling to be heard inside your head. I call these voices the Captain and the Kid. If you have ever flown on an airplane, then you can relate to this analogy.

> **THE CAPTAIN IS THE VOICE IN YOUR HEAD THAT TELLS YOU WHAT'S GOOD FOR YOU.**
> **THE KID IS THE VOICE IN YOUR HEAD THAT MAKES DOING WHAT'S GOOD FOR YOU DIFFICULT.**

The Captain flies according to the flight plan and speaks with calm authority when he comes over the intercom to make an announcement. He doesn't speak often, but when he does, it is to say something significant. He knows where he is going. He understands what is happening. He is ready to explain.

He is Order, personified.

You can easily ignore him.

The Kid, on the other hand, is the child who sits behind you every once in a while. He kicks the back of your seat. He talks constantly. He cries when he doesn't get his way. His crayons roll down the aisle beside you. He is always too loud.

He is Chaos, personified.

He is hard to ignore.

Take your experience with these two voices on an airplane, and apply them to your thoughts. The Captain and the Kid are influencing how you approach every aspect of authorship, and I know that understanding their influence will be a revelation that brings breakthrough. But for now, think of these two voices in the simplest way.

The Captain is the voice in your head that tells you what's good for you.

The Kid is the voice in your head that makes doing what's good for you difficult.

So if you are similar to my former high school students and starting to feel that strong urge to skip the outline, then please return to your seat and keep your belt buckled. There is turbulence ahead. We will land this plane, but not before we are at our final destination. Until then, let me caution you to listen closely to the voice that's suggesting a shortcut. Is your Captain speaking? Or is it the Kid? Here's how to recognize the difference:

The Captain will ask you to be patient and have some protein.

The Kid will try to convince you to pour syrup straight into your mouth.

So when the Kid gets loud, reassure him that he can have the chocolate.

But only after the chicken.

9
STRUCTURE YOUR CHAPTERS

THE PRINCIPAL LAUGHED UNTIL TEARS wet his cheeks. I sat across from him, blinking. I couldn't see what was so funny. I had just finished my first year of teaching high school English to sophomores who struggled academically. Some dealt with food insecurity and worked jobs to help pay basic bills for their families. Others didn't even have families; they caught a couch to sleep on wherever they could find one—with friends or friends of friends. I started bringing a bag of apples to school, and made it available to any students who couldn't concentrate because they were hungry.

They were struggling academically because they had no structure in their lives. They never knew if the electricity was going to be turned off, or if their mother was going to be arrested. Surprises had started to sting. So I tried to make my classroom routines obvious and expected, by writing the same things on the board each day and greeting students in the hall in the same way.

But there had to be something more I could do for my second year of teaching. How could I make every action and visual in my classroom so predictable that only the academic content itself was a surprise, and a nice one, at that?

As I reflected on my rookie year, I remembered how much they had paid attention to my clothes. I tend to wear bright colors with a quirky style. At times, it was distracting to my students, and they would ask a lot of questions about my shoes or shirt.

So what if I wore the same thing everyday? That provides repeating structure, right?

Feeling a burst of inspiration, I ordered five pairs of khaki pants, five short-sleeved button-down shirts with my initials monogrammed on the pocket, a black sweater vest, and black Mary Jane shoes. Then I made an appointment with my principal on the last day of the school year.

"I want you to know that I will be wearing the same thing every day next year," I told him, going into detail about why I think repeating structure would support their learning.

That's when he laughed.

When he saw the confused look on my face, he wiped his eyes and took a breath.

"Look, I'm really sorry; I thought you were kidding, Nika. Your clothes don't provide repeating structure. In fact, I think wearing the same thing every day might be more distracting than you think. Listen, you have had a great first year of teaching, keep trying to create repeating structure for your students. But do it with your procedures, not your outfit."

A couple days later, my new "uniforms" came in the mail. Because I was scheduled to teach six weeks of summer school to seventh graders, I decided to try my repeating clothes theory on them: I wore khaki pants and a white shirt with black sweater vest every single day.

Boy, was it a flop.

The students kept asking me if I were ever going to wash my clothes, and in one team meeting, my fellow summer school teachers held an intervention and asked me if I was in need of financial assistance.

My principal was right.

But so was I. People learn best when they know what to expect. Repeating structure allows your reader to relax and receive new information.

You just don't have to have a capsule wardrobe to provide it.

THIS IS THE REPEATING STRUCTURE OF A TYPICAL RESTAURANT:

1. Host welcomes your party and asks how many will be dining.
2. Host checks floor plan for availability and pulls correct amount of menus from a bin.

3. Your party follows the host to a particular table, and everyone takes their seats.
4. Server welcomes your party and takes your beverage and appetizer orders.
5. Server walks away for a brief amount of time, and your party studies the menus.
6. Server returns with beverages and appetizers then offers to take your entree orders or give you more time.
7. Server walks away for a longer amount of time after taking entree orders.
8. Server returns to deliver entrees and ask if you need anything else, periodically checking on your party for the next half hour.
9. Server returns to ask if you would like dessert or the check.
10. Eventually, your party pays the bill and leaves the restaurant, thanking the staff on your way out.

THIS IS THE REPEATING STRUCTURE OF A TYPICAL LIVING ROOM CLEAN-UP:
1. You toss any trash.
2. You take dirty dishes to the kitchen sink.
3. You straighten pillows and throw blankets.
4. You dust surfaces.
5. You vacuum or sweep the floor.
6. You light a candle or spray room freshener.

THIS IS THE REPEATING STRUCTURE OF A TYPICAL CHURCH SERVICE:
1. Church members walk into the building, greeting one another.
2. Worship leaders in the sanctuary begin a set of three songs, and members join in singing.
3. Associate pastor leads a prayer and communion, inviting members to bring their tithes and offerings.
4. Worship leaders begin another song.
5. Associate pastor makes general announcements.

6. Lead pastor delivers a biblical message.
7. Associate pastor closes the service with a prayer and an invitation to come forward for repentance or prayer.

THIS IS THE REPEATING STRUCTURE OF A TYPICAL BEDTIME ROUTINE:
1. You take off your day clothes and put on pajamas.
2. You wash your face and remove make-up, following up with moisturizer.
3. You brush your hair and brush your teeth.
4. You pull back the covers and climb into bed.
5. You read a book, talk with your spouse, or watch TV until you are ready to turn out the light.

The details of these scenarios can change, but the basics are the same. People like patterns. We like knowing what to expect at a restaurant, at church, and in other public places. We like doing the same things when we approach tasks like cleaning and daily routines. You can plug different specifics into the repeating structure without changing the basic order.

In the restaurant, the server may be a middle-aged woman named Jan or a teenaged boy named Jason. It doesn't matter. There may be five in your dinner party or just two. You may order a burger or you may order enchilada soup. Plug the specifics into the repeating structure.

In the living room, you can have twenty pillows or two. You can have no dishes that day or the paper plates and confetti from a holiday bash. You can light a cinnamon candle or a lavender one. Plug the specifics into the repeating structure.

In the church, you can attend on a week night or on Sunday morning. You can sing hymns or modern songs with a band. You can give your tithe on a phone app or in a collection box. Plug the specifics into the repeating structure.

In the bedtime routine, you can sleep in flannel pajamas or an old college t-shirt. You can brush your teeth with minty toothpaste from a tube or a homemade batch of baking soda, salt, and essential oil. You can read a fiction book or watch the news. Plug the specifics into the repeating structure.

I am about to share my favorite secret to book writing. Seriously, I believe this will unlock an aha moment for you that would enable you to complete your manuscript with joy. If you do the work I am about to show you, this one decision will be worth every bit of your investment of time, money, and effort to read this book.

Here is the first part of the secret. Not only does your book need an outline, but your chapters need an outline, too. I call it your RCS, your **repeating chapter structure**. If you can create a repeating structure for your chapters, then it will allow you to move through writing them with relative ease. All you have to do is plug the specifics into the structure.

How do you create a repeating chapter structure? You ask yourself the key elements that you want to include in each chapter.

How many teaching sections will there be?

How many stories?

How many Bible verses?

Any questions, reflections, or responses for the reader to fill?

Pull all of these elements into an RCS that will be the pulse of your manuscript. I should emphasize that sometimes these chapter structure elements are obvious because there are bold section headers, but they do not have to be. In most books, they won't be seen by the reader, but they will be felt and sensed.

An example of a chapter structure that is seen by the reader is in one of my client's books, *Navigating Motherhood* by Becky Brooks. When Becky and I were working together to create a detailed outline for her manuscript, we decided that she would adhere to a repeating chapter structure like this:

1. Family Story
2. You-Are-Here Question (with blanks—interactive for reader)
3. Bible Lesson
4. Drop-a-Pin Verse

5. Direction Question (with blanks—interactive for reader)
6. Prayer Prompt (with blanks—interactive for reader)

Navigating Motherhood: Finding Your Way by Following Jesus is a 12-week devotional for mothers at any age or stage, so it made sense to make the repeating chapter structure visible to the reader. The bolded words in the RCS were actually printed as recognizable headings within the book. The RCS is obvious. And if Becky had tried to write this book straight from a blank page without planning a detailed outline first, she would have been overwhelmed. Her book is 12 weeks with five devotionals in each week. That is 60 devotionals, and it means she planned her detailed outline by plugging in these specifics:

1. 60 Family Stories
2. **60 You-Are-Here Questions**
3. 60 Bible Lessons
4. **60 Drop-a-Pin Verses**
5. 60 Direction Questions
6. **60 Prayer Prompts**

Without creating her repeating chapter structure, Becky would have been completely lost in her manuscript, as if she were leaving on a trans-Atlantic cruise without a compass. But once she knew where to plug the specifics into the structure, she found such a big project to be doable.

Still difficult, but doable.

In another client's book, *Help Her Be Brave: Discovering Your Place in the Pro-Love Movement* by Amy Ford, the RCS does not show so easily. *Help Her Be Brave* is a call-to-action for churches to know how to respond with support and love when a mother with an unwanted pregnancy chooses life. Amy and I created a repeating chapter structure that looked like:

1. A Girl's Story
2. What the Bible Has to Say
3. Discovering Your Place
4. What It Looks Like for Her
5. Practical Ideas and Resources

This RCS does not require interaction from the reader. There are no blanks to fill in. But Amy found it refreshing to plug the specifics into the structure as she prepared her outline. There were ten chapters, so Amy picked ten girls' stories, ten Bible passages, ten ways churches can discover their place, ten more girls' stories, and ten lists of practical ideas and resources.

Both Becky and Amy spent a significant amount of time and effort to create their RSC, but as soon after they did, the writing of the manuscript was simply a matter of weaving together the different parts. They knew they had enough information to make their message last until the last page.

Have you ever read a book that kind of faded out? I experience one every now and then. The writer started strong and put all of their best stories and insights in the first half of the book … but then they ran out of steam in the second half. That tells me that they did not create a detailed outline. They may have made their way through Levels 1, 2, and 3, but they never got to details. They stopped at knowing the chapter titles.

You have to get to the details if you want to have a book that goes all the way from the beginning to the end.

Luke 14:28-30 comes to mind every time I encounter a new author who wants to start writing quickly without creating an RCS. It reads, "For which of you, intending to build a tower, does not sit down first and count the cost, whether he has enough to finish it—lest, after he has laid the foundation, and is not able to finish, all who see it begin to mock him, saying, 'This man began to build and was not able to finish'" (ESV)?

You have to prove to yourself that you have enough content to complete the manuscript or you will not have the stamina to do it.

You can create your RCS in the downloadable workbook.

Now that you understand one important part of my writing system—creating an RCS—please lean in while I share the next part. Next, you will commit to your chapter length.

In a previous chapter, I helped you determine a word count goal for your entire manuscript, perhaps around 50,000 words. Now look at your outline. How many chapters do you have? Keep in mind that you will also probably have an introduction and conclusion in your book, so you can add those to the outline. Count each chapter on the outline, including the introduction and conclusion.

Take your word count goal for your completed manuscript. Then divide your word count goal by your number of chapters. There is a page in the downloadable workbook that you can use for this.

Our example writer, Kaycie, has 12 chapters in her outline, and her word count goal for her entire book is 50,000 words. That leads her to a total of 4,166 words per chapter. Now she has a **Chapter Word Count Goal**. Just like Kaycie, when you follow this equation, you will have a very valuable piece of information—your chapter word count goal, a smaller measure to attain.

So many people have asked me how long a chapter should be or how they can know when they are finished with a chapter. Maybe you have wondered this too. Now, this is just my opinion, and it is not fact, so please do not take what I say as set in stone. Plenty of wonderful writers do not adhere to the next guideline I am going to share with you. But I am completely sold on it for myself, and I would be remiss not to offer this advice to you.

I think chapters should be close to *even* in length and presented in manageable chunks, not too long. I think it brings a sense of balance to the reader. So I would avoid one chapter that is very long followed by another chapter that is short, followed by another that is medium length. I would keep the chapter length balanced.

And I recommend that the perfect chapter length is between 1,500-2,500 words. So if you divided your word count goal by your number of chapters and came up with a chapter word count goal that is less than 2,000, then you may have too many chapters, and you could combine a few concepts. But if you ended up with a chapter word count goal that is greater than 3,000, then you might not have enough chapters, and you could break your topic down into smaller increments so you can add more chapters.

In other words, if I were Kaycie's book coach, I would balk at a chapter length of more than 4,000 words and advise her to cut those chapters in half and divide the points in her outline further. With 24 chapters instead of 12, her chapter length would be 2,083 words, and that is more comfortable to a reader.

Voila! You have so much information now, and a blank page is no longer a bully. You know the repeating structure in each chapter in your manuscript, and you can plug in the specifics. On top of that, you have a word count goal for each chapter, which means when it is time to weave the specifics into a cohesive and readable chapter, you will have a clear guide for how much is too much and how much is not enough. No more guesswork.

AS YOU TAKE ON THIS PART OF YOUR BOOK CREATION, KEEP REMINDING YOURSELF THAT THIS IS WHAT YOU WANTED.

As you take on this part of your book creation, keep reminding yourself that this is what you wanted. This is especially important if you have an RCS like Becky Brooks's that requires 60 of everything. During the days when we were working in intense coaching sessions of writing and editing, She often had tears in her eyes. Ironically, she was almost experiencing birth pains as she wrote *Navigating Motherhood*. I had to keep reminding her that the delivery would be worth the difficulty. So she bit her lip and kept writing.

But if you do not have a book coach, how do you stay motivated?

My friend and fellow life coach, Lea Ann Slotkin is the artist who painted the gorgeous image of flowers on the front cover of this book. Once, we were talking about how we often feel unmotivated to show up and attend to the basic tasks of creativity when there are no immediate rewards from the work. Plenty of time, there are no readers, no buyers, no interest, no gallery guests, and no applause. But we must work anyway.

"On those days I give myself a pep talk," she told me. "I think to myself, *Before you complain or quit, take a minute to remember what Little Lea Ann wanted. She wanted to be an artist. So let her keep doing it.*"

While you work on your detailed outline, you will feel birth pains, but it will help to bite your lip and remember what Little You wanted.

You wanted to be a writer.

Let Little You keep doing it.

10

FORMAT YOUR MANUSCRIPT

THE BEST I CAN DO IS A CASSEROLE. If you come to my house for dinner, please don't expect beef bourguignon or shrimp scampi or anything involving multiple measuring cups. The main ingredient in our meal will be a can of cream of chicken soup, lovingly poured out for you.

Maybe it is because I have a disability, but when I move around in the kitchen too long, I feel like I am going to faint. Don't get me wrong, I can stay steady at a podium, speaking for two hours or longer. But 20 minutes back and forth from the sink to the stove, and I'm spent.

Every now and then, I dream about having a sous-chef. You know, that person who prepares every little bowl for the main personality on cooking shows. All Rachael Ray or Bobby Flay have to do is show up and smile, tossing around tiny pre-measured condiments and swiping previously-chopped vegetables or meat into a mixing bowl. Now, I know they are experts and designed the recipes in the first place, but still, somebody else did the pre-work.

All they do is mix it all up into a meal.

Can you imagine if, every time you were ready for a meal, you simply walked up to the counter and the ingredients were all laid out for you in little bowls?

As it is now, when it comes time to eat, I open the refrigerator door and stare. Then I open the pantry door and stare. Then I leave, getting in the car so I can pick up a meal.

It's the Blank Page Effect, but on a plate.

Have you experienced The Blank Page Effect? It comes time to write. You open your laptop and stare. Then you open the Bible and stare. Then you look for inspiration online and stare. Then you leave, getting in another frame of mind so you can pick up your self-esteem.

But wait! What if you had a sous-chef?

What if someone went before you and pre-measured, pre-chopped, pre-seasoned, and prepared all those little bowls? What if all you had to do was toss it all in and mix it up?

That is the effect of formatting your manuscript the way I am going to teach you.

I call this method your **Heat Map Manuscript**.

Here is the long and short of it. You are going to enter your Level 3 Outline, with your RCS filled out in detail, into your writing software of choice (Google Docs, Microsoft Word, Scrivener, etc). If technology is a breeze for you, this will not be a problem. But if you tend to experience technology as an obstacle, please do not throw your hands in despair or drop your hands in defeat. Do not even entertain the thought that you are behind or overwhelmed. If cardiologists can do open-heart surgery, we writers can format a manuscript. It is just part of

Second Timothy 1:7 tells us the truth about times we feel overwhelmed. It says, "God has not given us a spirit of timidity, but one of power, of love, and of a sound mind." What will give you a sound mind is the peace of God. You have to keep coming back to your security and identity in Him. He is your willing partner.

And so am I.

Read on to discover my philosophy of how to use a Heat Map Manuscript, and when you are ready to create yours, I have prepared several templates and an instructional video that you can access at www.nikamaples.com/manuscript. In it, I will teach you everything from the standard font size to the placement of headers and footers. You need to know the basics of formatting your manuscript because we won't be using the pretty fonts you might be drawn to. Never fear. I'll show you what to do, dear writer.

But first, adopt the philosophy of what we will be doing as we format.

Simply put, a heat map is a visual representation of heightened activity. The higher the temperature, the warmer the colors on the spectrum: yellow, orange, and red. The lower the temperature, the cooler the colors on the spectrum: green and blue. This image of a heat map is what comes to mind when I think about writing a book.

When I was a novice writer, I would sit down to write, and because of an experience I had the day before—maybe a billboard or story or scripture caught my attention—I was eager to write about something specific. For instance, one time I saw a young golden retriever jumping and chasing butterflies, and it was doing it playfully, not with any real intent to catch or eat them. The butterflies were not flying away from him, either; they seemed to play back.

Oh, I had such a burning desire to write about this scene, and I knew the perfect chapter where it could go! It felt like a moment of Holy Spirit highlighting. He had shown me something truly special. The only problem was, when I sat down to write, the temperature in my heart was high, but there was no heat map on my laptop screen. The place where I would tell my story about the dog and the butterflies would not come until Chapter 10, and I was on Chapter 2.

Immediately, I felt deflated. I did not want to write Chapter 2. When I thought about Chapter 2, the temperature in my heart was ice cold, yet the cursor was blinking, begging me to begin. I shut the laptop and walked away. And the story I had been so ready to write was never written, only because it wasn't time yet.

I knew there had to be a solution. What if I developed a simple technique that would bend time for writers, making any part of their working document available to them any moment that they felt the temperature rise?

And so I created the Heat Map Manuscript.

If you do the hard work of filling in every detail of the repeating chapter structure in your Level 3 Outline, then place it in your writing software and follow the simple steps I show you in the instructional video found at www.nikamaples.com/manuscript, then you will be ready to write anything the Holy Spirit highlights for you on any given day. A regular manuscript becomes a Heat Map Manuscript when the elements of the outline are made into clickable links that take you precisely to that spot in the document and back again.

You will no longer have to move through your manuscript in a linear or sequential order. The sections and chapters in your outline become clickable links that help you navigate within your document with ease. This means, when the temperature in your heart is high for a particular topic, but you are on Chapter 7 and you had planned to write about that in Chapter 24, there is a solution. You just click on Chapter 24 and write. Tomorrow you may want to write Chapter 12. The next day, you may want to go back to Chapter 7. You write where the Holy-Spirit heat is. You never have to push yourself through places that feel cold. And you will have a clear way to get anywhere you need to go. You will not know how valuable that is until you have written a document that is 200 pages or more. Finding a paragraph in a 50-page document is doable. But you will get lost in 200 pages if you don't have a map.

YOU NEVER HAVE TO BE BULLIED BY A BLANK PAGE.

This book is called *Page One to Page Done*, but I didn't write it that way. I didn't move from one chapter to the next. I followed the Lord in and out of this message like a playful puppy chasing butterflies. I wrote wherever I felt passion and had Spirit-inspiration.

I meant what I said. You never have to be bullied by a blank page again.

When you have taken the time to create a Heat Map Manuscript, it's the closest thing to having a sous-chef. The English teacher inside of me is cringing because I am mixing metaphors here, but I am going ahead with it.

As an author, there has been nothing more helpful than sitting down and finding all of the little bowls of measured ingredients prepared before me. Creating my Level 3 Outline with detailed RCS and the clickable links of a Heat Map Manuscript is like having a sous-chef.

All I do is mix it all up into a manuscript.

It's like I'm the Rachael Ray of the page.

You can think of formatting your manuscript as preparing a place for your words. But what about preparing a place for ... *yourself*? There is another aspect of your writing that I wouldn't want to overlook: your writing space.

One of the biggest hang ups for writers is having somewhere to write. I have met many people who stalled because they wanted to create a perfect space to write. They wanted to paint the walls and make it a place of peace and productivity. Another version of this obsession is acquiring the ideal equipment. I have met writers who came to me for coaching, but then they would not begin writing until they had a modern, up-to-date laptop.

Although novelist Virginia Woolf did famously write, "A woman must have money and a room of her own if she is to write fiction," this is a well-intentioned myth. You do not need the perfect place, and you do not need the ideal equipment. Only once—for a brief time—have I had an office, and I almost never wrote in there! There were too many expectations when I walked into the room, and I felt pressured.

So where do I write? Well, right now, I am writing from the kitchen table. But I frequently write in libraries, in coffee shops, in church lobbies (some are open throughout the week and are quiet and peaceful), and I even write on my friend's beautiful back porch at times. Long ago, I asked her if I could drop by from time to time and write there for a few hours. She didn't mind, and I am thankful for the open invitation. I also write on my living room couch, but for me, I often need to get out of the house and visit one of the places I just listed.

It is possible that having the perfect place could be a detriment, not a benefit. One of the problems of having a dedicated office for writing is that you become dependent on it, and won't be able to write anywhere else. So why not avoid that, and just train yourself to write anywhere? Basically, I am willing to write a book anywhere that I would read a book, and I have decided that my flexibility is a benefit.

Speaking of reading ... Will you consider for a moment that it is a bit pretentious to require a perfect place to write, when your reader, the one whom you are serving, does not always enjoy the luxury of a perfect place to read? Sure, we would all enjoy being wrapped in a cozy blanket by the fire while we read ... or to be rocked in a hammock by salty beach breezes while we read ...

Yes, that would be perfect.

But it is likely that the reader you are serving will not be in their perfect place while they read your book. Instead, your reader may be holding your book in one hand and feeding a baby with the other, or riding on a grimy subway on their hour-long commute at the end of a terrible work day, or heaven forbid, your reader may be reading your book beside a hospital bed while their loved one sleeps fitfully. Dare I say that if our readers can endure discomfort, we can too? We are writing for the Kingdom, which is harvest work, and there are times when our muscles will be sore and our fingernails muddy. Kingdom work is heavenly, but that does not mean it is perfect.

It means it's worship.

Regarding the computer situation, I hope you won't wait for the ideal equipment, either. I wrote my first two books on a laptop that was so old that it often shut down and erased everything I had just written. The letter *D* did not work. But I kept writing on it because I couldn't afford anything else. And do you know where I got my next laptop? I'm talking about the really stellar one that I used to write three more books?

Get ready for this.

A reader who had read the first two books sent me an anonymous gift card to an electronics store and encouraged me to buy a new computer.

An actual reader reached out and asked for more!

What if I had never written those two first books on the old crummy computer? I wouldn't have been able to touch that reader, and they would not have been able to bless me with what I needed.

I thought I needed equipment before I could do the work, but like so many aspects of my writing career, the opposite was true.

The work had to come first.

> **KINGDOM WORK IS HEAVENLY,
> BUT THAT DOES NOT MEAN IT'S PERFECT.
> IT MEANS IT'S WORSHIP.**

Select your writing places based on what you feel, not what you see. Sure, you can seek peaceful, quiet, generally clutter-free atmospheres that are orderly when you can, but don't try to find one perfect place. Pick places where you feel possibility. That's all you really need. A few pleasant options to choose from will be just fine. When you show up, God will bring everything else.

Matthew 6:25-33 reads, "Don't worry about your life, what you will eat or drink or about your body, what you will wear. Is not life more than food and the body more than clothes? ... For your Heavenly Father knows you need these things. But seek first his kingdom and his righteousness and all these things will be given to you as well" (NKJV).

There are some things you can do to make a difference in any humble environment where you are, and they don't involve spending money. For instance, you can and should pray prayers of cleansing and blessing over every wall and surface in the room, as you lay hands on them. But let go of the decor, for now. It doesn't have to be just right in order to write.

Walls that are prayed over are much more beneficial than walls that are painted.

Still unsettled about your space? It was during a time of feeling concerned about creating a perfect place for me to write that I came across Isaiah 66:1, which reads "Heaven is my throne and the earth is my footstool. Where is the house you will build for me? Where will my resting place be?"

And this one:

First Corinthians 3:16 tells us, "Don't you know that you yourselves are God's temple and that God's Spirit dwells in your midst?"

I wonder what would happen in our lives if, instead of focusing on preparing the environment to be the perfect place for us to write, we focused on preparing ourselves to be the perfect place for God to write through us?

Then we could be *His* sous-chefs, and when He was ready to do something powerful in our lives, all He would take our little bowls of persistent faith, fresh humility, and fervent prayers that we have set before Him.

Then He'd mix it all up into a miracle.

11

CHOOSE YOUR VOICE

MY APARTMENT WAS A LONG WAY from the parking lot and the dumpster. The sidewalk I had to use to get to my front door was beside a busy boulevard. On most days, this didn't bother me, but if the weather wasn't ideal, I would resent it. I didn't like carrying groceries so far on a rainy day or lugging trash bags while trekking over the icy pavement. But walking was not the only thing irritating me. I also was getting tired of climbing up a flight of stairs and of not having a porch or patio to enjoy when the weather was nice.

When my lease was up, I decided to move.

Before I began looking for a new apartment, I made a list of the things that were important to me:

    1. An attached garage
    2. A nearby dumpster
    3. A patio
    4. The first floor

After checking out several apartment websites, I didn't know where I'd like to tour. A few places had two of the features I wanted, other complexes had the other two.

Over and over, I would compare one apartment to another, asking myself, "Should I go with this one or that one?" I was spinning in indecision, creating a quagmire in my mind.

Finally, I decided not to make a decision about every apartment on its own, instead of putting them side-by-side. I asked myself the same question about each location.

Apartment A: Is it a complete yes or a complete no if there were no other apartments to compare it to or choose from?
Apartment B: Is it a complete yes or a complete no if there were no other apartments to compare it to or choose from?
Apartment C: Is it a complete yes or a complete no if there were no other apartments to compare it to or choose from?
Apartment D: Is it a complete yes or a complete no if there were no other apartments to compare it to or choose from?
Apartment E: Is it a complete yes or a complete no if there were no other apartments to compare it to or choose from?

Come to find out, I had only two yeses to work with, not five. Well, that made it a bit easier. I called the two complexes that were yeses and made appointments to tour. After the tours, I followed the same decision-making process.

Apartment B: Is it a complete yes or a complete no if there were no other apartments to compare it to or choose from?
Apartment E: Is it a complete yes or a complete no if there were no other apartments to compare it to or choose from?

By approaching my decision this way, I chose Apartment E fairly easily, and it taught me a new principle about choice: Decisions made from comparison instead of completion create confusion.

It will simplify your life to choose as if each option were all there is. Would you say yes or no to that thing, if it were the only thing available?

Put that principle in your pocket as you move forward with your Kingdom-focused writing project. Writers have to be decision makers. Every detail in a book is a decision, and if you are someone who doesn't like making decisions, then finishing your book is going to take a long time and be quite uncomfortable. Get good at decision-making, and you will sail right through.

Making decisions is about committing to a risk. That's right, as one of my own coaches, Myron Golden, says, "Everything's a guess until it's tested." We want a guarantee, but the best we can do is a guess. So stop waiting and hoping that someone will tell you if you are making the right choice. They don't know the answer. Nobody does. Just guess and then test.

One obstacle that makes it difficult for new writers to make decisions without asking over and over, "Is this right?" is something called **imposter syndrome**. Imposter syndrome is the feeling that you are not equipped or qualified to write a book, and if you ever tried, one day people would find out that you are a fraud. So you might as well not start.

Now where do you think a thought like that would come from? There is only one place. In John 15:13 Jesus says, "You did not choose me, but I chose you and appointed you that you should go and bear fruit and that your fruit should abide, so that whatever you ask the Father in my name, he may give it to you" (ESV).

God says you are chosen and appointed. That is the truth. So we know imposter syndrome doesn't come from Him. And anything that is not coming from your Creator should not be considered. Even for a moment.

GOD SAYS YOU ARE CHOSEN AND APPOINTED. THAT IS THE TRUTH.

Imposter syndrome comes from the enemy. And everything that comes from the enemy is a lie. Here is a question worth pondering: "Why is it easier to believe a lie than the truth?"

Be aware that the opposite of imposter syndrome is not pride. It is service. That gives you a clue as to why the enemy would try so hard to work imposter syndrome into your thought patterns. It is because he doesn't want you to serve.

If you see your book as your way to serve, you will do it whether you feel qualified or not. If you saw a child on the playground fall face down in the dirt, you would run without hesitating and serve. You'd help them stand again. You wouldn't stop to ask yourself if you were qualified to help. Not for a second. You see someone who needs help, and you help. You don't help in a perfect way. You help in your own way.

As I have said, personal experience is your qualification. And personal style is your communication. In writing, **voice** is the display of that personal style. Voice doesn't just happen accidentally. It is the result of a series of choices that are made before and during writing. The voice of your book is its personality, and it has four parts: perspective, point of view, tone, and mood.

Your book's voice will reflect your own so you must learn to value your voice. Discovering that your voice has value is a critical realization. If you do not fully understand that you are the right person to write this book, you will miss the essential element of voice in your writing.

There are two reasons we hesitate to value our voice. The first is that we are afraid that we really do not know enough and the other is that we are afraid of appearing prideful.

To address the first hesitation, just accept the fact that there will always be people who know more. But if you know anything at all, you should share it. To do otherwise is selfish.

To address the second hesitation, it is not prideful to want to contribute what you have learned, admitting (internally, not in a public announcement) that God chose you to offer help in this area or on this topic.

Jeremiah 1:5 says, "Before I formed you in the womb I knew you, and before you were born I consecrated you; I appointed you a prophet to the nations." If we look closely at what

God said about the prophet Jeremiah and apply it to ourselves, we can see that Jeremiah couldn't take credit for his position or words of wisdom. He was chosen before he was born. That means he couldn't have done anything to earn the position of prophet. And we can't either. Indulging in feelings of imposter syndrome is a waste of what God already has embedded in us.

PERSPECTIVE

Let me affirm that you are the right person to write this book. The intersection of your experiences and the Holy Spirit's insight is your **perspective**, and it is from there that you serve. Your perspective matters because you are the only person on earth who has had the unique set of circumstances you have had. Other people may have had similar lives, but no one has had the exact same life that you have had, and as a result, no one sees the world exactly the same way you do. Even identical twins have differing perspectives of life because God has a relationship with each of them as individuals.

POINT OF VIEW

The term **point of view** is different from perspective, although it seems similar. As I've said, perspective is the intersection of your experiences and the Holy Spirit's insight. Point of view is the vantage point from which your perspective is shared.

Specifically, point of view (POV) involves the part of speech called pronouns.

If you are writing your book from your POV, you will often use the pronoun *I*, which is called **First person**.

If you are writing your book from the reader's POV, you will often use the pronoun *you*, which is called **Second person**.

If you are writing your book from an impersonal or narrator's POV, you will often use the pronouns *he*, *she*, *it*, or *they*, which is called **Third person**.

First person is best for memoirs.

Second person is best for Self-Help. I am writing the how-to book you are reading right now in second person.

Third person is best for informative writing.

All of the pronouns will be used throughout your piece. But what is the main pronoun you will choose for your perspective? To help you choose, think about the answer to this question: What is your nearness to or distance from a topic, and what is your reader's nearness to or distance from the topic?

With first person, you are closer to a topic than your reader is.

With second person, your reader is closer to a topic than you are. (In the case of this book, it is your own project you are writing, after all. You are closer to it than I am.)

With third person, you and your reader are equal distances from a topic.

TONE AND MOOD

Remember that I said a book's voice is its personality? How do you know a person's personality? Isn't one way that you can see a person's personality is through how they choose to dress? Some people dress in a consistently formal or put-together way. Others dress in a natural and casual way. Some dress in an unique or artistic way. People show who they are through their choice of clothing. A book is very similar. Its personality can be seen in how it dresses.

Playing "the dress-up game" is the best way to determine the voice in a piece of writing. There is a page in the downloadable workbook where you can imagine your book's style of clothing, if it were a person. What is your writing style for this particular project? (By the way, your voice can change from project to project. You commit to one style or voice per project. You do not commit to one style or voice for your entire writing career.)

Is your book's personality formal or casual? Is it serious or humorous? Is it calm or aggressive? Is it familiar or funky? Is it quirky or classic?

There is no right or wrong answer. It depends on what your reader would want. Would your reader respond best to writing that sounded highly educated? Then including humor might not be a good idea. Would your reader be put off by writing that comes across as stuffy?

Then humor might be the ticket.

I have found that one way to convey a book's personality is through **contractions**. You don't realize it, but all day long, you are making subconscious decisions about when to contract words. You'll remember from high school English that contractions are two words that are shortened and joined together.

Contractions are casual, that's all there is to it. So the number of contractions you use determines how casual your book feels. Think about your life. The same exact sentence, with the same exact words, comes across differently when some of those words are contracted.

For instance, I wanted *Twelve Clean Pages* to be a bit formal. So I was careful not to use contractions when I could avoid it. But I wanted *Hunting Hope* to be approachable. So I didn't hold myself back from using contractions.

In choosing the kind of "clothes" our book would wear and whether we would use many or few contractions as we write, we are creating the **tone** and **mood** of our project. Tone and mood can be differentiated simply.

The tone of the writing is the attitude of the writer as they write.

The mood of the writing is the feeling of the reader as they read.

Think of it this way. Imagine two different middle-aged writers are writing books for young college students interested in becoming lawyers. Both of these writers had been interns at the same law firm during the same year. One writer felt successful because his work was appreciated. Immediately upon finishing his internship, he began working for a prestigious law firm, of which he later became a partner. And then he became a judge. He'd had a wonderful career.

The other writer felt discouraged because his work was criticized. Immediately after finishing his internship, he interviewed at more than 25 law firms, and finally was hired by the firm he liked the least. No one else had given him an offer. He'd had a miserable career.

These two writers would create books with distinctly different tones. That is because they have different attitudes toward the role of an internship and the hiring process for lawyers. In that case, their readers would experience a very different mood in both books.

Readers of the first book would say, "You should read this book! It is so inspiring and makes me feel hopeful!"

Readers of the second book would say, "You should read this book. It is sobering and makes me feel cautious."

When we say a book is dark, fun, encouraging, sad, scary, and so on, we are describing mood. The author's tone made us feel that way. And they chose their tone on purpose so they would communicate clearly.

There is no concrete answer when it comes to your book's voice. The selection of perspective, point of view, tone, and mood amounts to a few hunches that must be acted upon, not labored over. Don't piddle around with these decisions for too long, hoping the right answer will strike you. It won't.

This isn't difficult, really. Here, I will echo the slightly sarcastic words of John Cusack in the 1989 romantic comedy, *Say Anything*, "How hard is it just to decide to be in a good mood and then be in a good mood?"

In case your mother never gave you permission, I'm here to give it to you: You can just smile and decide things. Leave second-guessing behind forever. Now go and prosper.

You may be asking why I have emphasized decision-making so much in this chapter. Because it is absolutely essential to increase your confidence in this basic skill if you are going to be an author. No one wants to read a book written by someone who was spinning in indecision the whole time.

What I am about to say sounds far-fetched, but again and again, I've found it to be true: Emotion is conveyed through the page.

That means whatever you feel while you are writing your book is what your reader will feel while they are reading it. So if you are spinning in indecision as you write, that is going to come across loud and clear, and your reader won't trust you.

Because they can tell you don't trust yourself.

12

UNDERSTAND YOUR EXPECTATIONS

THE WORK YOU NEED TO DO in this chapter is the kind of thoughtful and prayerful wrestling that happens between you and the Lord alone. There's not much I can teach you about you. That's His job. Yet I want to suggest something that you may not have considered. Expectations are the heart-hidden deep things of writing a book that most people never discuss or consider. No writing teacher would lead with this lesson because it would scare off the new folks. But I am the kind of friend who will tell you when you have spinach in your teeth or toilet paper stuck to your shoe. So let's do this thing, shall we? Please join me on a leisurely walk through the minefield of your expectations.

Eventually, everyone will get to this place, and for some, it will be too late. But not you. Let's start with the difference between **expectations** and **consequences**.

Friend, there will be consequences when you publish your book. In fact, there may be consequences simply because you are attempting to write one. Consequences in and of themselves are neutral. The word consequence has two parts: *con*, meaning *with*, and *sequence*, meaning, well … *sequence*. A consequence is neither positive nor negative. It is something that happens within the sequence. When you publish a book, you are starting a sequence. Some of what follows within the sequence will be good consequences; some will be bad consequences. Right now, let's consider whether you can avoid some of the consequences that would be bad.

Pray and ask the Lord for His guidance and help. Then ask yourself these questions and really spend time listening to Him and thinking about the answers below the surface. Some of the questions may not apply to the topic you are writing about, but most writers include some reference to their personal lives, even if they are not writing a memoir, so ask anyway. There is a page in the downloadable workbook where you can record your answers.

1. Have I forgiven and fully healed?
2. Would the person I'm writing about be harmed or hurt?
3. Would the people connected to the person I am writing about be harmed or hurt?
4. Is it possible that I will regret this later?
5. Am I willing to let the person I'm writing about or people connected to them read with veto power in advance?

That last one made you shudder, didn't it? I know; I'm with you. But I would never ask you to do anything I have not done myself, and this is what veto power looked like for me. When I finished the manuscript of my memoir, *Twelve Clean Pages*, I had a strong sense that the Lord was wanting me to give my father the first copy of the manuscript, along with veto power on any of its contents.

More than once, I prayed, "Do I have to?"

As much as I hoped it would, the Heavenly Whisper never changed. So I knew I was supposed to show my father my words. That felt extremely vulnerable because as I was telling my life story in the book, I had been honest about our difficult relationship and how it changed after my parents divorced. My biggest fear was that I would give him the manuscript, and he would say I couldn't publish any of it. In obedience to God, I would have honored my father by calling off the project, but it would have hurt my heart.

Sometime around Christmas that year, I gave him the manuscript, along with a gift card to a local restaurant. I asked him if he would read my memoir, knowing the whole time that I was giving him veto power. I proposed that we discuss it over dinner when he was finished.

An entire year passed, and I heard nothing.

Finally, I called him the following Christmas and told him that I wanted to publish my manuscript and needed to know his thoughts before I moved forward. He told me that I was free to do so.

Through tears that night, I cried out to God, "Why did you make me do that? It felt humiliating!"

God replied, "Now give your brother veto power."

I did not want to give my brother or anyone else veto power. I wanted to scream.

But God loves us more than we love ourselves, and He knew what I needed. So I gave my brother my manuscript, and we all read it aloud together as a family. Out of 71,000 words, he only vetoed two paragraphs.

The first paragraph that he vetoed was a scene when I was teaching high school English, and a student in my class had said a curse word. I had included it in the dialogue to maintain realism. Mark said no. Looking back, I wonder why I disputed him and defended my right to use a curse word in my book, if I were quoting someone.

"Look, one day, many people will read this book," he said, "and some of them will be very young. You want every reader to focus on what God has done in your life. You do not want them to be distracted by one, random curse word. It has no place. And I think it is something you will regret printing in a book with your name on the cover."

I accepted my brother's veto, and deleted the phrase that included the word.

The second paragraph that my brother vetoed was a description about my father that was disrespectful. Again, I argued. I really liked the metaphor and poetic words I had chosen in that section. Mark said no. Looking back, I wonder why I fought him a little and insisted on using the gift of words that the Lord has given me to take a jab at another person and thereby grieve Him.

I accepted my brother's veto and deleted the entire paragraph that both dishonored my father and dishonored my Father.

To this day, I could not be more grateful for Mark's wisdom and willingness to stand on his convictions. He was right—I would have deeply regretted publishing a book with my name on the cover and those two ugly paragraphs inside. That's not who I want to be.

So hear my admonition from where I am standing, just ahead of you. Let someone you trust have veto power. Ask the Lord who it should be. There are some things in your book that you will not be able to see without outside help, and the Lord knows it. He told us in Proverbs 15:22, "Plans fail for lack of counsel, but with many advisers they succeed."

If you want to succeed, don't go into the publishing industry with guns blazing like some Lone Ranger. The consequences are fierce, and you won't make it out alive without sufficient backup.

After you consider the consequences, what's next?

Expectations are just as important. Almost no one measures their expectations before they begin writing a book, yet everyone has them. I want to alert you to the possibility that your expectations can hurt you if you are not careful. Once again, I say that based upon my own experiences.

Expectations are imagined consequences that never happen.

One more time, please pray and ask the Lord to direct your thoughts. Then answer the following questions.

1. Have I surrendered the outcome of this project to the Lord?
2. Do I have someone specific in mind who I would like to read this book?
3. Have I imagined a scenario involving monetary relief or a sudden increase in income?
4. Am I thinking my life will change significantly?
5. Have I been hoping that this project will elevate others' perception of me?

I implore you to seriously address these questions with the Lord because it is your responsibility not to hurt yourself. People's reactions to your book will not hurt you. Your expectations of their reactions will hurt you.

For me, there were always specific people I hoped would read my books and appreciate me or think highly of me. I wanted certain people to love my book, and I truly thought they would.

But then they never read it.

Or they read it, and their reaction was, "Meh."

You think it won't happen, but it will. And when it happens, it won't mean that your friends and family don't love you. It could mean all kinds of things. But all of the things it means are about them, not you. The reactions of other people are always about them and what's going on in their lives and in their minds and in their hearts at the time.

But expectations are about what's going on in yours.

It's best to let go of them now. Your book might change a lot of people's lives, but probably not the people closest to you because you stand to gain something from their change, and that hardly ever works. Like I said at the beginning of this chapter, you can't teach a person anything new about them. That's God's job.

Let Him do it.

13

WRITE YOUR MANUSCRIPT

THE RACE OFFICIALS HAD TAKEN DOWN all of the balloons and half of the finish line counting device by the time I arrived. The rest of the runners had finished The Cowtown 5K in less than 45 minutes. But I had come in at 1:45. I may have finished an entire hour later than everyone else, but I had determined that the wheels on my walker were going to wear out and quit before I was.

It is worth noting that other than the first three finishers, all the hundreds who ran the Cowtown 5K that day have the exact same reward: a medal, hanging from a ribbon. I got to take home a medal too, even though I barely had a finish line left to record my time at the end of the race.

Let my 5K experience remind you that the reward of a completed book is worth it, no matter how long it takes you to get there. So once you start writing, please don't quit. Trust me, the water you drink at the end of a finished race tastes so much sweeter than the water you drink after you've walked away from an unfinished course.

So before the starting gun fires, it might encourage you to hear my perspective on endurance as an experienced writer. My logged experience as an author makes me a double-master.

In his book *Outliers*, Malcolm Gladwell explains that it takes 10,000 hours of practice to master a given skill. If you were to amass 10,000 hours of experience, it would take about ten years—if you practiced five hours per day. Yet, I believe you can get to the point of mastery faster if you write with the following intentions, offered to you by a coach who is well past 20,000 hours of writing practice.

The idea is just to write, again and again and again. I love the straightforward command in Habakkuk 2:2, when God told the prophet, "Write the vision and make it plain on tablets that he may run who reads it" (NKJV). If we want people to take our ideas and run with them, we have to make them plain on tablets.

Or on keyboards, as the case may be.

Before you begin, understand that there are three steps, and three steps only, to finishing a manuscript:

1. **CREATE A DETAILED OUTLINE.**
2. **SCHEDULE WRITING TIME.**
3. **WRITE DURING WRITING TIME.**

We just spent the first 12 chapters of this book on number one. Regarding number two, there is no need to be stringent when scheduling writing time. If you have never had a regular writing time before, it is not likely that penciling in a two-hour writing time six days per week is going to work for you. Habits take time to build. So start with something much smaller. You can either schedule a longer writing time once per week or schedule a micro writing time more often. The person who writes for two hours every Thursday will make the same progress as the person who writes for 20 minutes, six days per week.

It's the same amount of time.

The important thing is that you commit to yourself that you won't berate yourself if you miss a writing appointment. Remember, I'm the founder of Team No Streaks, and anyone is welcome to join. Over my 28 years of author experience, I have never flawlessly kept my writing commitments, and I am fine with that. One of my clients recently said, "I have decided to allow my values to interrupt my intentions. I can schedule a writing time, but if my son calls and asks me to come over and watch my granddaughter, I drop everything and go. One of my highest values is my presence and availability as a grandmother. I allow that value to interrupt my intention of writing."

I agree with her. I allow my values to interrupt my intentions. That means sometimes, I write every day. Other times, I write once a month. But I never punish myself for not writing because I don't try to write from willpower.

I've already proposed the problems of relying on willpower, but I think it bears repeating, lest you find yourself in the quicksand of it as you begin to write.

People think willpower is motivated by self-discipline, but it's not. Will power is motivated by self-punishment. Willpower says, "If you don't do this, you will be sorry."

You can't will yourself to do anything you don't wish to do. Willpower is a joy drainer because you start to hate anything that promises to punish you. Negative thoughts and emotions become attached to your writing, and then you avoid it even more. People may do things—but they won't do things well—under the threat of punishment.

Wishpower is different. Wishpower is a joy giver because it promises to reward you. When you desire something, you do whatever it takes to have it. The more you visualize the result you desire and experience the feelings you expect to have when you achieve that result, the more you will marinate in those positive emotions. Positive emotions will become attached to your writing, and you will want to show up for it even more. And the more you show up for it, the more you guarantee your success.

That is a fact based upon the biblical principle of The Law of the Harvest.

YOU CAN'T WILL YOURSELF TO DO ANYTHING YOU DON'T WISH TO DO.

One of my favorite verses in the Bible is Galatians 6:9, which reads, "Let us not become weary in doing good, for at the proper time, we will reap a harvest if we don't give up."

That sounds like a guarantee to me. God doesn't promise when the harvest will come, but He promises that it will. The Law of the Harvest is the very concept that motivated Christ to finish the work of salvation. Hebrews 12:2 tells us, *"For the joy set before him* he endured the cross, scorning its shame, and sat down at the right hand of the throne of God" (emphasis mine).

Jesus didn't self-punish His way to Calvary. He didn't endure voluntary crucifixion by willpower. I don't think that would have been enough to see him through. But He could see what was waiting on the other side of His suffering, and for the joy set before Him, He kept going.

The same thing will keep you going.

So decide right now that you will not waste time in beating yourself up for missed writing appointments. Support yourself and be kind. And if you find yourself unmotivated to write, please realize that you must be running low on wishpower. The only reason anyone does anything is because they feel like it, and you have stopped feeling like writing. So go spend some time meditating on the joy set before you—your future results. Focus on the reasons you are moving toward those results and the feelings you expect to feel when you get them.

When you start to slow down, it's time to refuel your wish tank.

You can even create minute moments of desire within the writing process, and I have found that extremely helpful. For instance, if you stop a writing session when you are almost, but not quite, finished with the chapter or section, then you will create the impetus to come back to it. Make sure you jot down a few notes to make sure you can come back with the same intention, but leave the passage just short of done. That way, when you return to your work, you will not be bullied by a blank page. You will simply tie the satin bow on the passage you left open during the previous writing session and then move on.

Another way to do this is to finish the passage, but then plant a question that will stimulate your thinking the next time you write. Ideally, the question will lead into the next passage. Leaving a passage just short of done or planting a question for yourself are ways of leaving an "open loop." The human brain cannot tolerate an open loop. We always come back to close it.

WHEN YOU START TO SLOW DOWN, IT'S TIME TO REFUEL YOUR WISH TANK.

Personally, I have found The Pomodoro Technique to be a useful tool in leaving open loops and keeping me writing. The Pomodoro Techique is a time management practice developed by Francesco Cirillo in the late 1980s. Cirillo used a tomato-shaped kitchen timer to time his intervals of focused work and stretch breaks in college. He would focus on his work for 25 minutes, followed by a five-minute break. After four, focused intervals (called pomodoros (the Italian word for tomato) and three breaks. The fourth break would be longer—maybe 15 minutes. Then the whole cycle would begin again.

When I write, The Pomodoro Technique is critical to my progress. Now, I typically set the time for longer pomodoros—usually 45 minutes—but for many years, the shorter focused intervals were highly effective for me. To help you get used to The Pomodoro Technique, I have created several pomodoro writing sessions on my YouTube channel, some with different lengths of time and different kinds of white noise to facilitate your writing time. You can check it out and pick a few favorites to come back to again and again.

Three other tools that I rely on as I write are Open Bible (www.openbible.info), Bible Gateway (www.biblegateway.com), and Bible Hub (www.biblehub.com). In recent years, there hasn't been a writing session when I haven't had all three open on my browser. I use Open Bible as a source of inspiration, Bible Gateway as a source of clarification, and Bible Hub as a source of calibration.

Open Bible is a wiki, meaning it is an open source document online. People all over the world have connected scriptures to themes. If I am looking for several scriptures on the theme of forgiveness, let's say, then I might turn to Open Bible and ask what the Bible says about "forgiveness." A long list of scriptures will come up, many of them without the word "forgiveness" in the scripture but centered on the theme of forgiveness, just the same. As I said, this inspires me to look into verses that I might not have thought of, otherwise. Bear in mind that this *is* a wiki, and do not forget it. It is not any more permanent or reliable than Wikipedia. For me, Open Bible is just a place I go to find a collection of verses into which I will look more closely.

Bible Gateway is one of the first places I go after I have found a verse of interest on Open Bible. On Bible Gateway, I will look up the verse, then use the parallel feature to view the verse in several translations, which I always view in order from word-for-word translation on the left to paraphrase on the right. On the word-for-word end of the translation spectrum, I might read from the King James Version or the English Standard Version. On the paraphrase end, I might read from the New Living Translation or The Message. I do this so that I can get an overall feel for the passage, considering the differences I see between versions.

Bible Hub is a free library of all kinds of theological tools, and is of immense value to the writer. When I want to study a verse, I can get lost in Bible Hub, consulting Strong's Concordance and countless commentaries. There is no excuse not to do your due diligence to understand the original intent of a biblical passage when Bible Hub is available to you at no cost.

With tools like these at your fingertips, you will have everything you need to keep writing. The key is to write—and only write—during writing time. Scrolling social media or switching the laundry are not the only deterrents to writing, either. Christians typically get sidetracked by a temptation much less obvious: praise and prayer.

That's right, when a Christian sits down to write, I've noticed that the knee-jerk response is to turn on worship music or bow our heads to pray. Perhaps we feel it is what we are supposed to do, as Christian writers. However, many clients have told me how they can get sidetracked by praise and prayer, and then they look up and 45 minutes have passed without so much as a word being typed into their document. I can assure you that what is acceptable for a writer would not work for another profession.

Christian heart surgeons cannot do anything other than operate during operating time. You wouldn't want your surgeon to lose your peak moments of anesthesia because he is singing a hymn.

Christian attorneys cannot do anything other than litigate during court time. You wouldn't want your lawyer to lose your only moments before the judge because she is on her knees in silent prayer.

I could go on and on. Christians in all other professions must pray and praise *before* the moment of truth, not during it. Why should it be any different for writers?

You must write during writing time. If you do, you are guaranteed to finish your book.

My friend Steven is an artist, and ten years ago, he started posting a daily piece of art on Facebook that we all started to anticipate joyfully. With a black marker, he drew a meaningful image on the side of a paper coffee cup. Some had the look of political cartoons, complete with social commentary. Others were inspirational. All of them were charming.

What we didn't know is that he was keeping all of the cups.

Then one day, in celebration of his tenth anniversary of creating cups, he changed his profile picture to a photo of him sitting in front of all 3,000 of them.

I can't stop thinking about that picture. If someone had shown Steven that massive collection ten years ago, and told him to go create it, I'm sure he would have felt overwhelmed and never started the task. But because he only tried to be faithful to complete one cup each day, he was able to do it.

It reminds me of the time I was writing the manuscript for *Keep Teaching*, a 365-day devotional for teachers. By the time I finished the third day, I wanted to quit.

How am I ever going to write 362 more of these?! It will take forever! I whined to myself.

Then, as if my ninth grade math teacher had walked into the room, I stopped complaining just long enough for the algebra to become clear. *Actually, it won't take forever to do this. If I write one devotional entry every day, it will only take me one year to finish. And if I write two entries every day, it will only take me six months. And if I write four entries every day, it will only take me three months!*

So that is exactly what I did. I wrote four entries every day and finished a 365-day devotional in just three months. I will always be glad for that sudden lightbulb moment that led me to make the impossible quite possible in my mind.

That's where the struggle is, you know. It's all in your mind. Your obstacles are not circumstantial so let the "nouns" off the hook. In other words, it's never the fault of people, places, or things.

Remember when I told you about the Captain and the Kid? Well, they are going to make a lot of noise when you start to write. The Captain is going to want you to stick with the flight plan and stay in the chair with your laptop open and fingers on keys. The Kid is going to want you to pay attention to everything else.

The apostle Paul let us know about the Captain and the Kid thousands of years ago so this should come as no surprise to us. In Romans 8: 12-13, he writes, "Therefore, brothers and sisters, we have an obligation—but it is not to the flesh **(the Kid)**, to live according to it. For if you live according to the flesh **(the Kid)**, you will die; but if by the Spirit **(the Captain)** you put to death the misdeeds of the body **(the Kid)**, you will live." (Obviously the bold part is all me.)

You are under no obligation to obey the Kid. In the end, you will have to decide how you can best endure discomfort during writing time. The discomfort isn't going anywhere. It is just part of the process. You may have imagined that professional writers are always comfortable when they write, but that is not true. Professionals *expect* to encounter discomfort from time to time when we sit down to write.

We just write anyway.

14

CREATE YOUR READER EXPERIENCE

IN MY YEARS AS A HIGH SCHOOL TEACHER, I saw many students come and go. After they became adults, some would write to me, giving me brief updates on their lives or thanking me for being their teacher. Do you know what I started noticing in those emails? No student ever said, "I remember that one lesson you taught me."

No, they all said, "I remember that one story you told me."

And even though it has been years since I was in the classroom, most students I hear from or run into at the grocery store can recall specific details of the entertaining or moving stories I've told them. And here's the surprise: they even remembered the instruction hidden inside the story.

You see, I wanted to help my students with the lesson, but I had to learn how to hide my help in stories because the instruction by itself was going in one ear and out the other. But a story is something a student can hold onto. People forget instruction, but they remember inspiration.

When it comes to reaching your ideal reader, it is a smart idea to hide your help in stories so that they will remember what you have taught. Therefore, storytelling is an important part of creating your reader experience. When you tell a story, your words can create worlds for them.

Jeremiah 1:9-12 is a fantastic reminder of the power of your words: "Then the LORD reached out and touched my mouth and said, 'Look, I have put my words in your mouth! Today I appoint you to stand up against nations and kingdoms. Some you must uproot and tear down, destroy and overthrow. Others you must build up and plant'" (NLT).

You can use your words to tell stories that build up belief and tear down disbelief. Here are a few tips to become a better storyteller.

STORYTELLING TIP 1: *Write What You Know*

In college, I took two courses in writing at Harvard Summer School. I shouldn't have to tell you that an imaginative girl like me can get swept away by a summer in Cambridge, Massachusetts. Every week, my poetry professor held office hours and invited his students to come by anytime to receive feedback on our poems. Once I came by, and we had a chat. After a few moments of talking about my current writing in class, he asked what I wanted to do in the future. I told him that I had decided to apply to writing schools in the Northeast.

He put down his coffee cup slowly. "Nika," he said. "Write what you know. There are plenty of fantastic writing programs in Texas. You can write vividly about the place you have always lived so why would you move and try to write about someplace new that you don't even know that much about?"

"Because I am so … so … so inspired up here. I don't feel that way at home."

"Open your eyes to your home," he said. "You would never be able to describe Massachusetts with accuracy and specificity. But that is exactly how you would be able to describe Texas. Don't reject your roots. Write what you know."

Write what you know is a common writing maxim. I didn't understand what he meant at the time, but many years into my writing career, I do. *Write what you know* means you should be careful if you are trying to describe a setting outside of your familiarity. That doesn't mean you can't write about places and things you have never experienced. It just means, be careful when you do.

In addition to setting, be cautious when you attempt to describe the feelings or motivations of another person. Whether it be an individual or a group of people, it is dangerous to make absolute statements about something you have never experienced. Perhaps the easiest example to use here is women who write about a man's feelings and motivations. Or men who write about a woman's feelings and motivations. It rings hollow, right? If you have not experienced the exact thing you are trying to describe, then proceed with caution.

Better yet, write what you know.

STORYTELLING TIP 2: *Show, Don't Tell*

A good writer believes that their reader is smart and can figure out a few things for themselves. In fact, a reader enjoys reading because they like figuring things out. That is one of the things that makes reading fun for them. Only an amateur writer misses the point of reading and hands everything to the reader directly.

Readers do not want to be told what to think. That is why another common writing maxim is *Show, don't tell.*

Most of this "figuring out" happens in fractions of seconds in the subconscious mind of the reader. I'm not talking about big revelations, such as in a mystery novel. These are more like small description discoveries. Let me give a few examples.

> **TELL:**
>
> I was nervous as I gave my speech.
>
> **SHOW:**
>
> Stammering with every sentence, I clung to the podium, hoping no one would notice my shaking fingers.

In this example, there is a big difference between telling that someone is nervous and showing the things that happen when someone is nervous. The reader feels connected to the story and to the character when they can figure something out and subconsciously think, "I bet he is nervous! The same thing has happened to me, too!"

TELL:
> "Stop it right now!" my mother whispered across the pew.
> Joe and I could see that we embarrassed her when we quietly goofed off during church.

SHOW:
> "Stop it right now!" my mother whispered across the pew.
> Joe pinched my arm once more, and I kicked his ankle. We both looked over at her. Her face was a shade of red I'd only seen on a Corvette.

In this example, I am showing both the emotion the mother is feeling (embarrassed) and what the boys had been doing (goofing off).

TELL:
> Dorothy felt empathy for her husband. Sam had worked another long day.

SHOW:
> Dorothy walked into the living room and saw Sam had fallen asleep during the six o'clock news. Softly, she kissed his forehead and took the remote from his calloused hand to turn off the TV.

What showed Dorothy's empathy? Her soft kiss and effort to let him sleep longer. What showed Sam had worked a long day? His calloused hand and the fact that he had fallen asleep at 6 o'clock.

You might say, "I can see how that works with fiction, but what about nonfiction?"
    Well, as you tell stories from your own life, remember that you did not have a narrator explaining things as the moments unfolded in real time. You did the subconscious figuring out by yourself as you were experiencing it. No one came and stole the simple pleasure of discovery from you by telling you what to think.

You noticed your teacher was angry when you saw his furrowed brow.

You noticed the child was happy when you saw her skipping down the sidewalk.

You noticed the woman was ready to leave when she started fumbling for her keys before the conversation was over.

You noticed the older gentleman had been crying when you saw his red-rimmed eyes.

You noticed.

You noticed.

You *noticed*.

As a writer, it is your responsibility to show your reader every detail. Be specific.

Let them notice.

Let them notice.

Let them *notice*.

Instead of writing about fruit on the table, write about navel oranges in a silver bowl.

Instead of writing about the smell of grandmother's house, write about the comforting fragrance of soap and talcum powder.

Instead of writing about the beginning of a lovely sunset, write about pink like layers of cotton candy appearing in the sky.

Make your book about the experience you can offer to your reader. Offer them a chance to do some figuring out. They will enjoy it so much more.

STORYTELLING TIP 3: *Kill Your Darlings*

I never call one of my books "my baby." Books are not babies. Books are sheets of paper with ink on them, merely records of one person's ideas. Books do not have souls like babies do. Books are not created in the image of God like babies are. And when you and I are old and gray, our books will not take care of us, listen to us, or help us in our time of need … but I sure hope that real human babies will grow up and do all of those things.

As your coach, I implore you not to call your book your baby. Here is why. You are going to see your book beat up and abandoned and rejected. And if you start thinking of your book as your baby, then you won't be able to take it.

Your book will be beat up when you see people angry or hurt or unimpressed by it. They may give it low stars and poor reviews. All of those things have happened to me.

Your book will be abandoned when someone reads it and then sells it in a garage sale, donates it to a thrift store, or resells it online for a dollar. If you think your book is your baby, you will cry when you see a bunch of your babies on the shelf at a discount outlet or resale shop. All of those things have happened to me.

Your book will be rejected when people don't want to buy it, or when you give it to them, and they never read it. All of those things have happened to me.

It is not easy to keep smiling when someone walks up to your book table, looks at the back of your book, crinkles their nose and says, "Nah!" and walks away. If you think your book is your baby, you will crumple to the floor in tears.

It's just paper, friend. Let's not get this out of whack.

BOOKS ARE NOT "BABIES."

Please just think of your book as sheets of paper with ink on them, a record of your ideas. It doesn't matter what happens to any single one of them because there will always be other copies. And if someone doesn't like them, then they are not liking your ideas. So what? Welcome to life. Not everyone is going to like your ideas. Most people prefer their own.

Not thinking of your book as your baby is the beginning of freedom from another problem: Getting too attached to pieces of your writing during the writing process. It is a subtle form of pride to think you must shield your creation from all critique. When a writer is too attached to pieces of the writing within their manuscript and refuses to delete words, they are advised to *Kill your darlings*.

Kill your darlings means being willing to delete or remove a sentence or a paragraph or section or a page, or even a whole chapter that doesn't serve the reader. Maybe you want to keep it because it is beautiful and you are proud of it … but it is off-topic and has nothing to do with the story or is confusing. Perhaps early readers are suggesting that you remove it. You know in your heart that it doesn't fit, but you keep insisting that it must stay. That is when you know you probably have a darling, and you must kill it. A darling is a weed. It simply cannot be allowed to stay in the flowerbed.

This has happened to me numerous times. I have deleted entire chapters because they didn't fit, and I knew it. I thought they were beautiful so that was hard to do. I had to find a solution that was a little softer, something that would allow me to put my darlings to sleep without killing them. So I developed a concept I call a **book bank**.

This is my advice to you so that you will be able to remove writing that does not serve your reader. Make yourself a book bank. Create a second document, and always open it at the same time that you open your manuscript document. Then, every time that you have to kill a darling, put it to sleep instead. Just copy it, cut it out, and paste it into your book bank. I always give my book banks the title of the book they are from.

When I was working on *Hunting Hope*, I created a document called "Hunting Hope Bank," and whenever I cut a passage, I put it in that document. Inside the actual file, the book bank looks like chunks of writing that do not flow together. I put three asterisks between each chunk, so I can tell them apart. The book bank serves as a collection of writing that you can use later.

So don't be afraid to kill your darlings. They are only like Sleeping Beauty when she pricked her finger on the spinning wheel. It may have looked morbid, but she was only sleeping. The same can be true of your precious words. They are valuable. So put them in your book bank until later. Then give them a kiss at the right time, and your darlings may have a chance to wake up in a whole new world.

STORYTELLING TIP 4: *Avoid Purple Prose*

My first book, *Twelve Clean Pages*, makes me cringe a little. That is because the whole time I was writing it, I was trying to prove that I was a good writer. I wasn't just trying to draw attention to my testimony and to what the Lord had done in my life. I was also trying to draw attention to my writing. That is obvious because of the occasional interjection of flowery words. Now, I love a good thesaurus; I always have. But while I wrote *Twelve Clean Pages*, I kept a thesaurus beside me like it was my best friend. Every time I thought of a word, I would look it up and replace it with a bigger and more complex word, just because I could. I thought that was what a great writer is supposed to do.

My writing had a bad case of *purple prose*.

It is called purple prose when a writer forgets that the writing is supposed to draw attention to something else. It happens when the writing calls attention to … itself. Writing calls attention to itself when it is overly packed with words or uses words that are flamboyant and sentences that make the writing feel heavy.

You may have noticed that when I was telling you I was writing *Twelve Clean Pages* with a thesaurus at my hip, I did not say that I used the thesaurus to pick a bigger and better word. I said I picked a bigger and more *complex* word. Sometimes the first word that comes to your mind is the better word, and you should not replace it. In many cases, I discovered those words for the first time when I looked them up in the thesaurus. Be careful not to do this.

Over the years my readers have told me, "I loved *Twelve Clean Pages*!" I wish their comments had stopped there. But many times they continued on to say, "You must be really smart. You have such a huge vocabulary! I had to stop over and over again to look up the definitions of those words!"

I wanted to tell them, "I had to look up all those words, too!"

When you have to leave your writing to look up a word in a thesaurus, then it is likely your reader will have to leave your writing to look up a word in a dictionary, and you don't want that.

Here's how to avoid purple prose:

A. Keep your writing simple. Don't get too fancy. Write the same way you talk.

B. Don't use a thesaurus to replace a word unless you have already used that word too many times. Don't replace a decent word just because you can. It would be a shame if that first word had been the better word.

Still not convinced that you should avoid purple prose?

Imagine if one of your friends lavishly applied three completely different perfumes to herself every morning. How would you feel when you saw her coming?

Now, you get it. More is not always better.

Sometimes more just gives you a headache.

Download your workbook at
www.nikamaples.com/popd_workbook

STEP THREE

Revising & Editing

*There is a time for everything,
and a season for every activity under the heavens.*

Ecclesiastes 3:1 NIV

15

READ YOUR MANUSCRIPT

THE SCHOOL BELL ECHOED in the hallway, and every student in my classroom stood to their feet. "Remind me who you are," I said. They answered in unison:

> *I am a child of God,*
> *Made in the image of God,*
> *Created in Christ Jesus to do good works,*
> *Which He has prepared in advance for me to do.*

Somewhere in the middle of my teaching career, I had started asking my students to stand and make a declaration at the beginning of class. I had adopted the idea from my church, where every children's Bible class—from cradle roll to middle school—began with this declaration, based on Deuteronomy 31:

> *I am the head and not the tail,*
> *Above only and not beneath,*
> *I am blessed coming in,*
> *And blessed going out,*
> *And everything I put my hand to will prosper.*

Bible teachers were repeating these declarations at church to embed Kingdom identity into every child. Hearing their young voices declare truth with such confidence was moving, to say the least. I wanted the same for my students. In public schools, I had my classes repeat a generic statement that did not have direct references to Scripture. The confidence-building declarations were still meaningful. But when I started teaching Bible in a private Christian school, the speed governor came off, and I was able to put the pedal to the floor. I wrote a simple declaration based on Ephesians 2:10, one of my favorite verses. The trigger sentence, *Remind me who you are*, is one that I encouraged them to say to themselves in the mirror, well into their college years and beyond.

The image of a university student standing at the bathroom sink in the morning, holding a toothbrush in his hand, looking himself in the eye, and saying, "Remind me who you are," before reciting Ephesians 2:10 was enough to give me chills. I knew the effect of this confidence-building, identity-grounding habit could last their whole life long. It isn't the big things that change a generation. It is the little habits that grow belief.

I mention this here because I think it would help you to begin each day with a daily declaration, based on the Bible. It will prepare you for what comes next in the writing process: revising. You will need a strong sense of identity as you revise and edit.

In previous chapters, I explained that indecision drains you of energy and willpower drains you of joy. During the revising process, you will be tempted to look at your work beside the work of other writers and compare. But beware, comparison drains you of identity.

When you look at your work against the backdrop of other authors you love, you run the risk of trying to sound more like them and less like yourself. Lysa TerKeurst doesn't need an understudy. You won't be playing her role one day, should she get chicken pox and need to take the week off.

You are still going to be you. So be the best you.

As soon as you have finished writing your manuscript, I recommend that you set it aside and take a two-week break. You have not completed the climb, but you are no longer at the base of the mountain, either. You might as well enjoy your progress. Step away from your manuscript and pretend that you are sitting down on a boulder to rest and drink cool water from your canteen before you start hiking again. Look down and see how far you have come. Remember that first day when you had nothing but a blank page in front of you? You certainly aren't there anymore. Celebrate the accomplishment by breathing deeply and feeling pleased by what you've done.

> **DOING GOOD THINGS DOES NOT MAKE US GOOD.
> WE ARE GOOD SO WE DO GOOD THINGS.**

I caution against feeling proud of it. My perspective on feeling proud shifted suddenly when I heard a friend explain that he tried to catch himself when he started to tell his son that he was proud of him.

"One day, I noticed that God never said that to His son," my friend offered. "The Father said that He was pleased, not proud. In James 4:6, it says that 'God opposes the proud.' And Christians aren't supposed to play with things God opposes."

This view of pride had never occurred to me, but ever since, I have steered my vocabulary and heart posture away from it. I don't tell children that I am proud of them anymore. I tell them I am pleased with them. And I don't say that I am proud of myself. I say I am pleased with myself.

Is this concept new to you, too? I'm certainly not advocating a legalistic approach to language. You will not be struck by lightning if you tell someone that you are proud of them. But don't dismiss this idea too quickly, either. Let it sit and marinate in your spirit for a while. The more you read the Bible, the more it will become clear that God encourages pleasure and discourages pride.

Take pleasure in the accomplishment of having finished the first draft of your manuscript. Celebrate intentionally as you take your two-week break from writing. Just enjoy being pleased for a bit. There is nothing wrong with that.

Then start reinforcing your identity for the task of revision ahead of you. If writing the manuscript were like a major weight loss program, revising is the last ten pounds. You can't stop too soon or you'll go backward. And as long as I am making this weight loss analogy, I should say that one of the things that has always stopped me from reaching my goals on the scale is not reinforcing my identity.

See, the mindset that got me into a pattern of weight gain in the first place was an identity rooted in entitlement. It sounds ominous when I call it what it really is, but when played out in real life, it seems so harmless.

"I have been good all week so I can have this dessert."
"I have been stressed all day so I have earned a treat."
"I have a lot of work to do so I deserve a venti latte before I get back to it."

Do you see how I base all of the high-calorie "rewards" on my own merit? Do you do this, too? If you can insert the word *deserve* into any sentence that has a reward at the end, then you are babysitting a sense of entitlement in your heart.

Entitlement is the child whose parent is Pride.

When we think this way, it is an identity weakness that needs to be strengthened. We have forgotten who we are and Whose we are. We are God's offspring, and entitlement is not in our spiritual DNA.

Doing good things does not make us good.

We *are* good so we do good things.

You didn't finish your manuscript so you could get something from God. You finished your manuscript because of who He says you are. Take pleasure in your accomplishment because your identity is strong. You understand who you are in Christ, and that means that you are designed to create and serve. Does it make sense to go bananas, throw confetti, and call all your friends when you turn the key, and your car starts? Well, if it doesn't usually do what it is supposed to do, you might. In most cases, genuine appreciation is enough.

YOU WANT YOUR BRAIN TO GET USED TO TOUCHDOWN TERRITORY.

One time, I was watching a football game with my brother, and an NFL wide receiver did a well-rehearsed victory dance when he made a touchdown. You've seen this kind of thing, I'm sure. It wasn't a simple celebration, but a choreographed number that was a few seconds too long. The pride came off the player like steam.

As we watched, my brother said, "Come on, act like you've been there before!"

It was the first time I'd heard it so I couldn't help laughing.

"When you get to the end zone, act like you've been there before," is a quote attributed to Green Bay Packers coach Vince Lombardi in 1967.

All my business coaches have told me something similar. They say when you reach a significant income goal, it is better to act like it is no big deal, business as usual, par for the course. Celebrate, but celebrate calmly. The more you go crazy in the "end zone," the more you are communicating to your nervous system that this kind of thing is not typical for you, and your mindset will calibrate to that low expectation. It will be a long time before you reach the goal again. But act like it is common, and it will be.

Yes, you finished your manuscript. Celebrate, but celebrate calmly. Take pleasure, not pride, in the accomplishment.

Act like you've been here before.

You want your brain to get used to touchdown territory.

16

POLISH YOUR MANUSCRIPT

PART OF ME THOUGHT making art was going to be easier than writing. That's why I switched my major to art for one year in college. But by the time all my clothes were ruined by plaster, paint, glue, oil pastels, ceramic mud, and charcoal dust, I knew it wasn't easier. I wanted to collapse from exhaustion.

I wasn't worn out by the work.

I was worn out by my professors' opinions of my work.

See, there is this little word that they don't tell you about when you are signing up for your first art class in the registrar's office: *critique*.

The critique kicked my backside. I was expecting that we were all going to give compliments, hold hands, and sing campfire songs during critique sessions. But it's really more like the cutthroat finale of a cooking competition.

The art professors would hang all of our art on a gallery wall or arrange all of our sculptures on a display table and critique each piece. Every member of class would gather around in silence and wait for the guillotine. I wanted to crawl out of the back of the classroom like a snail leaving a shiny trail of shame. Come to think of it, that very well may have been their strategy. Critique gets rid of all the wannabe art students like me who thought art was supposed to be easy.

If it were a strategy, it worked.

I couldn't have been more grateful when I tripped over a high curb one day and fell to the concrete, breaking my elbow and causing a nauseating period of vertigo. I had to fly home from Nashville to Fort Worth to heal on bed rest, and the remainder of my critiques for the semester were typed up and sent to me by email. I was then able to experience my failure from the comfort of my own home, instead of in front of an audience of my peers.

I knew I belonged back in the mass communications department. Somehow, I could handle the critique of my writing more than I could of my art.

Please don't make my mistake of thinking there is a place where you can escape critique. I had tried to run from my professors' critique of my writing in Basic News, Broadcast 101, and Media Law, only to crash into more of it in 2D Design, 3D Design, and Ceramics 101.

So let this mass comm grad deliver the bad news: Critique is everywhere.

Bah-and-so-much-Humbug.

It is not possible to put something you've created into the world and expect people not to have opinions about it. They will. But there are ways we can polish and prepare what we are presenting. We can double-check our work before we turn it in.

That's why this chapter is here.

If you slept through high school English or were too distracted by sneaking glances at the cute quarterback in the corner, use the rest of this chapter as a reference for writing principles you may have forgotten. I'm just your friendly high school English teacher, offering a well-timed reminder of the basics. And I promise I won't make you stay in after-school detention.

Don't be tempted to flip past this chapter. Lean in.

In your second read-through of your manuscript, you should correct these common errors as much as you can.

SPACE:

Space is an important factor in your document. From beginning to end, space is your friend. People who have experience with visual art and painting already know this because they learn the interplay between positive and negative space. What is not there serves as a frame to highlight what is there. If a reader looks at a page that is dense, without space, they will not want to read it. Many will put the book aside without ever diving in. It just looks like too much. But if space breaks up the writing on the page, then the reader has an instant feeling that reading it will be doable. Writing without space feels like only inhaling breath. Writing with space feels like both inhaling and exhaling breath. It is refreshing to the reader.

Do you notice all of the paragraphing I have incorporated in the book you are reading right now? Sometimes, I even set apart one word or one sentence as a new paragraph. You need these small breaks within your writing and groups the thoughts on the page so that the reader can breathe in and breathe out the information.

Paragraphs create space.

Especially short paragraphs. (See what I did there?)

> **WRITING WITHOUT SPACE FEELS LIKE ONLY INHALING BREATH. WRITING WITH SPACE FEELS LIKE BOTH INHALING AND EXHALING.**

DIALOGUE:

You must make it very clear when people are talking. The goal is to keep the dialogue untangled. Your reader needs to know exactly who is saying what. They don't like slowing down and going back to reread. I have simplified the dialogue-writing process down to four key points.

1. THINKING– Thoughts are designated by italics, not quotation marks.

Example:

If he would ever stop talking to take a breath, I could tell him that he has spinach in his teeth, Erica thought.

2. INDENTING– Indent a new paragraph every time someone new is speaking.

Example:

The rock music was so loud it almost made the doors vibrate. Sheila walked down the hallway on a mission. "Peter, will you please turn that down?" she yelled over the bass guitar.

Peter lowered the volume long enough to answer, "I'm doing my math homework, mom."

"Can you please turn down the music, son? Our dinner guests will be here in 15 minutes," Shelia looked at her watch as she said it.

"Okay, I will, mom. But loud music helps me think!" he hollered back.

3. TAGGING– If you use a tagline, (which is that *he said / she said* indicator at the beginning or end of dialogue), a period changes to a comma. Question and exclamation marks stay the same.

Example:

The longer Sebastian waited to pop the question, the more the ring box felt like a burning coal in his pocket. "Maria, it is a lovely evening. Let's walk out on the veranda," he said, his voice already a little shaky.

"No, thank you. My allergies have been bothering me. I don't want to start sneezing." She never looked up from her dinner plate.

Sebastian stood. "Let's give it a try, dear. It is a full moon tonight, and you wouldn't want to miss it. Will you please come on the veranda with me?"

"Here we go again! Why do you always insist on having your way?!" Maria said, slamming down her fork.

This proposal was definitely not going the way Sebastian had pictured.

4. NOT TAGGING–Don't go crazy with speaking descriptions; the word *said* is usually enough unless another word enhances the way something is being spoken. And you can choose not to tag if there are only two people speaking in short sentences.

Example:

There was a crash outside the window. Poppy and Finn looked at one another and then at the clock on the wall. It was midnight. Poppy was first to break the silence. "What was that?" she whispered.

Finn leaned over and answered her quietly, "It sounded like the geranium pot on the porch. I think it just broke."

"Do you think someone is out there and kicked it over?"

"It could have been a cat."

"What should we do? Call 911?"

"Wait. Not yet. Let's see if we can hear anything else."

EMBEDDING QUOTATIONS:

There is another use of quotation marks that you will be using frequently. This is not for dialogue; it's for **embedded quotations**. When you embed quotations, you are borrowing another writer's or speaker's words in a reasonable way to support your own writing project. These can be words from something in print, such as a book, a poem, or an article. These quotations can also be words from something that is not in print, such as a video, a sermon, a radio broadcast, or a podcast.

The following is a brief lesson on how to embed quotations.

NUMBER ONE: Choose the quote. Be sure to write down everything you can about where you found it, including the name of the book, author, and page number. Or the website, episode name, and day you accessed it. Store this information as a list in another document. You will need to provide this to your editor later.

NUMBER TWO: When you are ready to use the quote in your writing project, you must embed it into your writing. It will not be in the middle of nowhere unless it is an epigraph, which is when a quote stands alone at the beginning of a chapter.

> **Here is a bad example:** (Notice how the quote stands alone and is separate from my writing and how I do not mention where it came from. I have put the quote in bold so that it would be more noticeable.)
>
> Doubt is not a disease or diagnosis that we must accept. Christians can engage in simple, active seeking to transform their doubt into honest faith. **"In progressive Christianity, doubt has become a badge of honor to bask in, rather than an obstacle to face and overcome."** In some cases, overcoming that obstacle of doubt leads to an even deeper faith than before.
>
> **Here is a good example:** (I have embedded the quote by seamlessly making it part of my writing. Notice that all I have to do is make the words flow together. I don't have to do

anything else except add quotation marks on either side of the quote. Also notice that the period—or any other punctuation mark at the end of the quote—will go inside the quotation marks.)

Doubt is not a disease or diagnosis that we must accept. Christians can engage in simple, active seeking to transform their doubt into honest faith. In her book *Another Gospel*, apologist Alisa Childers suggests that in modern times "**doubt has become a badge of honor to bask in, rather than an obstacle to face and overcome.**" In some cases, overcoming that obstacle of doubt leads to an even deeper faith than before.

PARALLEL STRUCTURE:

One writing technique that adds pizazz is **parallel structure**. Parallel structure can come up in several ways as you write. It usually adds clarity to the message. The only question you have to ask yourself is whether you are using it too often. Too much parallel structure looks like repetition. Here are some examples of reasons to use parallel structure.

1. LIST– If you start each bullet or number in a list in a certain way, start them all that way.

Here is a bad example:

- Open your mind to read the Bible as if you have never read it before.
- Write your thoughts as you read the Bible.
- Calling a friend to talk about what you have read in the Bible.
- Pray that the Lord will help you apply what you have read in the Bible.

Can you spot the bullet point that does not follow parallel structure? It is the third one. The word "calling" is a verb, but it does not fit the other verbs in the list. The writer could fix the problem by changing "calling" to "call." or they could fix the problem by changing all the other points to having *-ing* endings, like *opening, writing,* and *praying.* Either solution works. But whatever is done, all of the bullet points have to match. That is what it means to be parallel.

2. BEGINNING AND ENDING– You can use parallel structure at the beginning or ending of paragraphs. A classic example of this is Martin Luther King Jr.'s *I Have a Dream* speech. He employs parallel structure as an effective technique to emphasize his point. At first, he repeats, "We cannot be satisfied until …" again and again. Then he repeats "I have a dream that …" again and again. It is pleasing to the reader's eye to glance down the page and see parallel structure in paragraphs. But only if it is used intentionally. When the beginnings of paragraphs repeat unintentionally, readers think of it as amateurish.

3. EMPHASIS– You can use parallel structure within the same paragraph, for emphasis at the beginning of sentences.

> **Example:**
>
> The chili boiled over and continued to cook until the bottom of the pot was a quarter inch of beans burned black. For months, everything in the house smelled like char. The curtains stunk. The coach pillows stunk. The bedsheets stunk. The towels stunk. Even the clothes in the closets stunk, which is why Edgar did not get the job at Steele Systems Incorporated. "It was just a bad interview," he says. "No one wants to hire a man who smells like burnt chili."

THE FIRST FIVE WORDS:
The first five words of every chapter are important. I learned this when I self-published *Twelve Clean Pages*. When the designer typeset the manuscript, he sent it back to me with the first five words of every chapter in a bolder, more captivating font. They were even in all caps. I asked

him why he'd done it this way, and he pointed out that most books highlight the first five words by putting them in all caps, bold, or setting them in a different font. I had never noticed that in books before.

Here is the thing. If the first five words of every chapter are emphasized visually by the designer, then you need to pay attention to them and make sure they are different from your other chapters, every single time. That is why I have started conducting a **First Five Audit** on my manuscripts. It has proven to be a very helpful practice to improve my work. Every time I start a chapter, I write down the first five words on a sticky note, and keep a running list. If there are any repetitions of the first five words within the same manuscript, I make changes.

REPETITION:
You would be surprised how many times you use a certain word or phrase. There is never an excuse to keep repeating yourself as you write, which a reader finds really annoying. They get tired of it, fast. It is easiest enough to fix repetition if you find that you have done it.

I had a book coaching client recently who was using the same two phrases over and over in her manuscript. I mentioned the two phrases to her and asked her to try to avoid using them so much. She nodded and said she understood, but the manuscript did not reflect a change as she continued to write it.

For her own growth as a writer, I wanted her to see the writing habit she had created for herself. So I scheduled a read-aloud time with her, and was secretly crossing my fingers that she would notice for herself. The two phrases were "in the midst of" and "knit together." Over and over, she would repeat "in the midst of" concerning all kinds of things or "knit together" concerning others.

Within the first hour of our read-aloud, she turned to me, cringing. She said, "Why am I saying "in the midst of" over and over again?"

I just smiled. Later, she noticed "knit together" as well. I helped her use the Find and Replace function in her writing software to add some variety to her manuscript. You can look up a YouTube video about how to use the Find and Replace function in your writing software to change repetitive words and phrases effortlessly.

There you go. These are a few of the revisions I use regularly when I polish my manuscripts. This is not a complete collection, by any means. The kind of revisions I mention in this chapter do not address the fine details of revising, which are not really necessary for a new writer to focus on.

Please don't get bogged down by the minutiae. There are professional "cleaning crews" for that, and they are called **editors**. When you work with an editor, they will do the deep cleaning required before publication. Don't worry about your grammar. It's not permanent. It's like an old stain on the carpet.

Your editor can take care of it.

Right now, your job is still to make the bigger changes. Think of it as rearranging the furniture in your book.

You want your reader to have a comfortable place to sit when they arrive.

17

OFFER YOUR MANUSCRIPT

WHEN MY BROTHER WAS A SENIOR in high school, his team made it all the way to the state championship. There, they would face our long-time school rival. We had beat them during the regular season so we were favored to win the title game. We had all driven to Waco to watch them win in Baylor's football stadium on that frozen November night. It was so cold, you didn't even want to breathe in the frigid air, but watching the boys play warmed our hearts.

All four quarters, they gave it all they had.

But in the end, they lost, and we all followed the football bus back to Fort Worth in disappointment.

Months later, close to the time of graduation, the school held a fundraising auction of memorabilia from the year, and one of the items up for bid was the football used in the state game. It was signed by all the players on the team and was encased in a clear box for display.

Now, tell me, who wants a losing football?

No one except my mother. The auctioneer made the last call, and my mother was the only one who raised her hand. She paid $100 to buy the football that nobody wanted. She bid for the ball, and after being displayed in the living room for a while, she moved it to a shelf in the garage, where it stayed for years. In fact, I became so accustomed to seeing it that I never wondered what had motivated her to purchase it.

Almost 25 years later, I finally asked her.

She said, "I bought a losing ball because the boys fought hard, in the bitter cold, all the way to the buzzer." Her eyes were misty when she said it.

Battles for which we show up and fight, no matter the outcome, are worth celebrating. Faithfulness is a victory in itself. The team might have lost the state game that night, but hey, they came to the field with their whole hearts, and that's saying something. In a world of inaction, sometimes the evidence of taking action is something that belongs on display.

FAITHFULNESS IS A VICTORY IN ITSELF.

My brother and I used to watch *G.I. Joe* cartoons every day after school, and the final scene always said, "Now you know. And knowing is half the battle."

But Joe never said the rest of it. If knowing is half the battle, then showing up is the other half. You gotta do something with what you know.

You gotta show up.

Knowledge is nothing without action.

Or as we read in James 2:17, "… faith by itself, if it is not accompanied by action, is dead."

Dead? *Dead*?

Seems a bit extreme, James.

But he wasn't kidding. Imagine a bright red can of gasoline, sitting in the garage. That's some powerful fuel. It can really take you somewhere. But it never will unless you pour it into the gas tank of a car and ignite it. Just *having* gasoline doesn't do you any good. You have to put it to use. If you don't, then it's as good as dead. Actually, now that I think about it, that's incorrect. Gasoline that just sits there, unused, isn't dead. It's dangerous.

The same is true of faith.

Faith is fuel. And there's no point in having it if you never put it to use.

I'm sharing all of this with you because this is the part of the manuscript process where you show up for the skirmish. You have spent considerable time planning, developing, writing, and revising your message. But until now, you have not had to exercise your faith by putting it into action. You only *thought* you've been through the hard part. When you offer your manuscript to readers for the first time, it is the difference between practice and the playoffs.

You will feel like you have a lot on the line.

My advice for offering your manuscript to the world comes in two phases.

PHASE ONE: *Offer It to Your Early Readers*
Select a small team of early readers who are willing to give you feedback on your manuscript. Some people call these early readers your **beta readers**. They are the ones who will see your work in its raw form, before thorough editing.

Who should these early readers be? Well, that is up to you. I like to choose no fewer than five and no more than 12 people who can give reliable feedback. Fewer than five will not give you enough differing perspectives on what you have written. More than 12 will give you too many opinions and make it hard to apply their responses.

You might be tempted to choose family members and friends, but I have found that it is better to give your first draft to strangers or acquaintances. Family members and friends may go too easy on you and give you generic feedback like, "It's good," rather than offering meaningful critique. They also have something at stake. Their own emotions about your writing a book are factored into their reading of the manuscript. That may or may not be helpful.

Now, when I say not to make family members and friends your primary early readers, I want to be clear that I am not referring to the person you give veto power to, as I mentioned in a previous chapter. That person will most definitely be a family member or close friend who knows you and your story well. But, generally speaking, your early readers do not have to come from the category of those closest to you.

When I choose strangers or acquaintances for this role, I will either make a post on social media and ask for someone to volunteer to be an early reader, or I will ask friends if they have a friend who might be willing to volunteer.

More often than not, I choose acquaintances, rather than complete strangers. I do that by compiling a list of people who are similar to my ideal reader. In fact, you might even want to go back to the people that you interviewed during the stage when you were getting to know your ideal reader. They would be perfect to give you feedback.

After you have a general list, sort them by age or life station, trying to create as much variety as you can. I always attempt to get one reader from every decade: 20s, 30s, 40s, and so on. In the past, I have chosen one of my former students (now an adult), one of my professors from the past, my doctor's wife, and a friend of my sister-in-law's. Early readers are everywhere. You just have to be willing to think long and hard, make a list, pray over it, and then start asking.

Some people you ask will say no, and there is no reason to take this personally. They may be in a busy season and lack the time to give. They might be too intimidated by the idea of being an author's early reader; I've seen that happen quite a bit. Eventually, you will have some cooperation and can get started.

I usually take the digital file of my manuscript to an office store and have them print it, double-sided, and put it in a spiral binding. Depending on how long your manuscript is, this can be a significant expense. I always choose to give my readers a physical copy because I want them to sense the importance of what they are being asked to do. Also, when they see the hard copy right there in front of them, they are more likely to highlight, underline, and write in the margins for me to see.

The alternative is to send your readers a digital copy, and if you choose to do that, then I have a bit of advice. First, don't send them all the same link to a manuscript that has been saved in the cloud, such as in a Google Doc. It is distracting for readers to see that another reader is reading the same document at the same time they are. And it will become confusing if you allow everyone to make changes or suggestions within the same document. What a mess that would be.

Instead, make separate files for each reader. For instance, with the manuscript for this book, I might save it with file names like "Page One_Smith," "Page One_Jones," or "Page One_Baker" for each person. This goes for times when I am sending them a link to a collaborative document that is stored in the cloud, as well as when I am sending them a static file like a Microsoft Word document.

Whether I am delivering or mailing physical copies or emailing digital copies, I will always include a brief cover letter, thanking them for their time and insight. In this cover letter, I also invite them to write responses within the document. I make it clear that I do not expect them to edit the manuscript or find mistakes. That is what most people think you want them to do as early readers, and that intimidates them.

Make sure they know that this is a first draft, and there will be plenty of typos, misspellings, and grammatical errors. They are welcomed to mark those, if they want to, but it is not what is most important because you will have an editor handle that later. Emphasize that you want these early readers to give you their overall heart response.

Here are some questions you can ask them in your cover letter:

1. **What was the most compelling part of this book?**
2. **Where was it slow or boring?**
3. **What kind of person would you recommend to read this book?**
4. **Which concepts from this book were new to you?**

5. What can I improve?
6. What other books does this remind you of?
7. What do you wish I had included in this book?
8. How can you see this book being used in the future?
9. What podcasts, television, or radio shows do you think would be interested in featuring this book?
10. Would you be willing to connect me with any influential people you know who would be interested in this book?

These questions can also be sent to them in a digital questionnaire, like a Google Form. Whatever makes it easiest for them to respond will be a help to you.

Also make sure you include a due date in your cover letter. Let them know when you would like to receive their comments. Anywhere from three to six weeks is plenty of time for your early readers to get the job done, but not so long that they will forget about it completely. Because you have given them a due date, it makes it that much easier for you to send a quick reminder when there is one week left. If you do not set a specific due date, you will experience the awkward feeling of chasing down your manuscripts after it has already been way too long. That's embarrassing for everybody.

When I finally receive all of the responses, I start to look over them. I never, ever look at them until I have collected them all. Then, I open all of the copies at once (whether physical or digital) to the first page and see what everyone wrote. I move through the entire manuscript, page by page, applying the suggestions that I want to apply. You will find that some people will not like a certain paragraph that other people love, and you get to be the deciding factor about whether it stays or goes.

Author and literary agent Mary Demuth says, "You write a book on your knees," and I can't think of anything more true. In the same way that you prayed over the list of people who would be your early readers, you should pray over their comments. By now you know that you have to kill your darlings from time to time, so if your early feedback calls for it, and God confirms it through prayer, then do not hesitate.

Your first draft is by no means your best draft. Offer it up for revision, and watch it improve before your very eyes. Your early readers will see things that you cannot see. And your read-aloud readers will hear things you cannot hear.

PHASE TWO: *Offer It to Your Read-Aloud Readers*

My recommendation after you have applied all the changes from your early readers is to have another group read your manuscript aloud to you. This practice is the game-changer that will take your book from good to great. Every book I have written has been read aloud to me by my family. So far, they have been my only read-aloud readers. Your group does not have to be your family, but they need to be people who love you and are truly committed to your success.

To create a read-aloud group, I pick several possible dates on the calendar and reach out to three to four supportive people who might be willing to come over for a read-aloud. My books have always taken either a whole day or two half days to read. If you choose to break up the process into half days, I would make sure that the days are one after the other or no more than one week apart. You do not want to lose momentum or the memory of what was just read.

When you have a consensus about the day and time of the read-aloud, you can prepare for the day by getting physical copies of the now-revised manuscript for each person. You can also send them digital copies and ask them to bring their tablet or laptop to read along. It would be helpful to have sticky notes, highlighters, and pens for each person, as well. And in addition to preparing for the reading itself, you will want to plan a meal, snacks for breaks, and plenty of hot or cold beverages, as needed. Even a bowl of cough drops or peppermints would be nice to have on hand.

When the scheduled day arrives, you and your read-aloud group will rotate around the room and read one chapter each, pausing to discuss where necessary. Hearing your own words in another person's mouth will make the manuscript real to you. More importantly, you will listen to the places where your intended meaning didn't come across, and there is nothing more valuable than that. Take extensive notes during the reading. You will want to apply them to your work later.

Both before you begin your read-aloud and after you finish, you and your small group of supporters will want to pray over your Kingdom-focused writing project, asking God to speak and give you wisdom.

Because it's not really your voice you're listening for as you read, is it?

It's His.

18

REVISIT YOUR MANUSCRIPT

THE AUTUMN SUN WARMED the front porch, as I ate my lunch and watched the autumn leaves fall. I couldn't have asked for a more peaceful Sunday afternoon.

Moments later, I was screaming.

A bug had slipped into my shirt, and I could feel it making its way from the nape of my neck down my back. If I had been inside the house, I would have ripped off my shirt. But out on the porch, I was stuck. I wiggled. I shook the hem of my button-down. I smacked as far behind me as I could reach. But the crawling continued. By that time, I was convinced it was a spider.

When it came around my left shoulder blade and under my arm, I was able to catch the spider in a handful of fabric. It moved between my fingers, and I yelled, "A-ha! There is nowhere you can go now!"

Pinching as hard as I could, I mashed the bug between my fingers until I felt it stop moving. Satisfied, I stood up and waved the bottom of my shirt until the bug fell out, and I looked down.

There by my feet was a smushed ladybug.

What a lesson. So many of the things we are afraid of are based on what we imagine them to be, not what they really are. If I had known that it was a ladybug crawling in my shirt, I would have calmly guided it downward and out without the panic and kiss of death.

Writer, let me assure you that you have nothing to be afraid of when it is time to revisit your manuscript after it has been read by you, then your early readers, then your read-aloud readers. Your fourth and final read-through will be done after the manuscript has been thoroughly edited.

That's right. It's time to send your work to a professional editor.

But don't worry. Editors are as harmless as ladybugs. They love books and consider themselves "wordies." Most of them aren't writers themselves so they respect writers. There is nothing they enjoy more than being one of the first people on earth who gets to read a book that is going to make a big impact. Editors are in your corner.

EDITORS ARE AS HARMLESS AS LADYBUGS.

I can say that now, but it wasn't always the way I felt. I remember when I had my first experience with a professional editor. More than a month passed, and I still could not open the document she had sent back to me. I was nauseated every time I thought about taking a look at what she had written. I had just finished *Twelve Clean Pages*, and had sent it to a professional, paying her a flat fee of $850 to edit my 71,000 words. I didn't know if that was a good price or not. All I knew was that she had been recommended by a friend who was also an editor, and I trusted that friend. My hands had been shaking when I hit the send button.

After a few weeks, this editor I'd never met sent the finished file back to me.

And that is when I froze. The word "editor" felt so final to me. So authoritative. I assumed an editor knew best, and I was afraid she would tell me I had no business being an author.

So the edited file sat, unopened, on my computer desktop for days upon days.

Eventually the file had to be opened, or my book could not move forward so I called a friend and asked him to come over and sit beside me while I looked through her remarks. There were tears in my eyes when I opened my laptop. I almost winced.

Then I scrolled through every page, still shaking.

The first few chapters had a few grammar corrections. She caught typos, misspellings, and alerted me to a few details I didn't know. For instance, I didn't know that the term for the elevated hallway from an airplane to the airport gate was a jet bridge. I had used another, commonly used word for it that also happened to be trademarked. I didn't know that I was supposed to cite quotations in a certain way. I didn't know that I shouldn't use song lyrics because you have to pay royalties in order to print them.

When I finally came to the end of the document, I shrugged. It hadn't hurt that bad. In fact, it hadn't hurt at all. The entire process had taken about two hours, and I'd quickly been able to apply her suggestions and changes because I'd already done so much work to correct my words in the first three read-throughs.

That is the experience you can expect if you choose to self-publish your book. You will hire a freelance editor who will either ask for a flat fee or charge by the word to edit your work. You can find these editors in so many ways. Several times, I posted on Facebook that I was looking for a professional editor, and people would reach out to tell me that they knew someone. Other times, I have looked on websites for freelancers, such as Upwork (www.upwork.com) or Fiverr (www.fiverr.com).

There are several types of editors. Two common types are developmental editors and copy editors. **Developmental editors** take an overall view of the manuscript and help you make big moves to develop your message. They may suggest removing a chapter or adding a chapter. They may rearrange the content. They may add transitional paragraphs or sentences in key areas. A developmental editor is usually important to consult earlier in the writing process. By the time you have already offered your manuscript to readers, and they have said it is clear and understandable, then you no longer need a developmental editor. I have never used one for my self-published works.

A **copy editor** is the type of editor you will want to hire at this stage. They go through your manuscript, line by line, and make detailed corrections. Please be aware that they are not concerned with content. It doesn't matter to them if your book is "good" or "bad." That is the job of the developmental editor. All a copy editor wants to do is make sure there are no errors.

As I mentioned in a previous chapter, I think of editors as your partners in creating a welcoming, homey atmosphere for your readers. A developmental editor is like an interior designer, and a copy editor is like a deep cleaning crew. Ultimately, you are the one in charge of placing the furniture, but you need these partners, just the same. A copy editor will clean up every little spill and stain without trying to change the environment too much. However, a conscientious copy editor will make suggestions for you to rearrange things, if they really see the need, but the ideas in your manuscript are not their focus. Precise language is.

The step of hiring an editor is not one you will want to skip. After three read-throughs, you will be tempted to move forward without one more set of eyes. You'll be so sure that you have caught every error by now. But you haven't. Believe me, you haven't. I am quite confident of my skills with the English language, as a mass communications grad and high school English teacher. But even I overlook little mistakes. I've always been glad I hired an editor.

A DEVELOPMENTAL EDITOR IS LIKE AN INTERIOR DESIGNER, AND A COPY EDITOR IS LIKE A CLEANING CREW.

If you choose to be traditionally published, you will be assigned a copy editor. This person might be different from the acquisitions editor who accepted your manuscript to be published. The copy editor from a traditional publisher will mark the same things that a freelance copy editor will mark. In fact, some of the editors who work for traditional publishing houses *are* freelance editors, and are available to work on both traditionally-published and self-published books.

However, an editor at a traditional publishing house will also be adhering to the rules of the house. Every publishing house has a particular way they do things. For instance, with *Hunting Hope*, I wanted to write the possessive form of Jesus like this: "Jesus' arms are wide open," which is an acceptable way to punctuate *Jesus*. But my publisher said that their house standard was to write it like this: "Jesus's arms are wide open." When you are being published by someone else, you must yield to their preferences.

In *Hunting Hope*, the editor also had some theological questions based on what I had written. I was able to show biblical references for the statements I had made, and the two of us carried on a long discussion about how to word it in the best way, without leaving room for misunderstanding. When you are traditionally published, you cannot decide things for yourself. You and your editor must come to an agreement. But it is not like I first thought. Editors are not authoritarians who bring down the red pen and say, "And that's final!" You always have the opportunity to talk about their choices and yours.

However, when you self-publish your book, the choices—and the responsibility—are all yours. If you want to, you can reject every single one of the editor's suggestions. That probably wouldn't be a good idea, though.

After an editor at a traditional publishing house has made changes that you have applied, you will send the completed manuscript back one more time, and they will run it by two or three proofreaders. The proofreaders come in and look over the text one more time after it is typeset, a process I will explain in coming chapters. Proofreaders make sure that not single letter or punctuation mark is missing.

Even if you self publish, you will want to revisit your manuscript one more time after it is typeset, inviting proofreaders to read through it. By that time, it will be almost perfect, so it won't cost much to pay two to three proofreaders. That will be your fifth read-through.

You might be thinking, "*Five* read-throughs! I don't have time for that!"

And I would argue that you don't have time to do fewer than five read-throughs. Your book is a somewhat permanent thing, and you will not want to find errors that you could have avoided if you had only spent a little extra time and effort before publishing.

It's okay to be so tired of your own book by that point that you don't even want to look at it anymore. I've been there. But trust me, you will be more tired of hearing about the same typos over and over again for years to come because new readers keep finding it and sending you emails about it. It's worth it to take care of it now.

Besides, there is another reason to keep going over and over your content this way. Once you have read-through it five or more times, you will be very familiar with it, and that will serve you well when it is time for media interviews and other marketing. There have been so many times when I was being interviewed and was able to recall an exact phrase or was able to point to a specific place in my book because I had read it five times.

The editing process doesn't have to be big and scary. There are days you will want it to be over, but just keep coming back to the truth: It may be uncomfortable, but it won't hurt you. There is no need to react in terror.

Editors are as harmless as ladybugs.

Download your workbook at
www.nikamaples.com/popd_workbook

STEP FOUR

Publishing & Launching

The Lord gave the word: great was the company of those that published it.

Psalm 68:11 KJV

19

WRITE YOUR BOOK PROPOSAL

MY FAMILY LIVED IN A CENTURY-OLD HOUSE when I was quite young. Though it needed some repairs when they discovered it, my parents thought it was too good to pass up and purchased it anyway. Then my father climbed scaffolding every weekend for months to install new gray siding and maroon shutters. My mother tells me that the interior needed significant work, too, and she had to haul hot water from the kitchen to fill the bathtub for more than a year.

That Christmas, a special dollhouse awaited me under the tree.

My parents had found an unpainted dollhouse that resembled our home. My father had painted it gray with maroon shutters, just like our real house. Then my mother filled it with tiny furniture, some purchased and some homemade. They weren't really replicas of our life-sized furniture, but the resemblance was close enough to captivate me.

Our real house had a grandfather clock, and so did my dollhouse.

We had a record player, and so did my dollhouse.

The little father, mother, and daughter dolls were brunette. The son doll was blond. Just like our family. It all seemed so real to me.

Imagine if a guest had walked into our home for the first time and had seen me playing with my matching dollhouse on the living room floor. They might have assumed that the real house had come before the dollhouse, although I supposed there have been people who loved a dollhouse from their youth so much that they used it as inspiration to build their actual home.

Sometimes the dollhouse comes first, but most of the time the real house comes first.

You can think of a **book proposal** in a similar way. A book proposal is just a matching dollhouse, the miniature version of your manuscript.

A book proposal is necessary when a writer seeks traditional publication. It is not necessary for self-publishing. Even so, the occasional self-published writer may want to create a book proposal in order to understand and plan for their book in an extensive way. I drafted a book proposal for this self-published book, in fact.

For the purpose of this chapter, let's assume our writer Kaycie is seeking traditional publication for her book about Christlike leadership in public education. She knows she will need a book proposal in order to go that route.

Should Kaycie write her book proposal before she writes the full manuscript or after? Well, it depends.

If she hired me as her book coach, on our next coaching call, I would tell Kaycie that a book proposal comes first when the writer has already shown proficiency. This may have occurred in multiple ways:

1. THE BOOK PROPOSAL WILL COME FIRST WHEN THE BOOK IS NONFICTION, AND THE WRITER IS A CELEBRITY.

In this case, the literary agent and publisher will probably accept the book proposal without a completed manuscript. In the event that the celebrity does not have strong writing skills, they may hire a **ghost writer** or the publisher may assign one to the project. A ghost writer is someone who writes a manuscript on someone else's behalf. Some ghost writers receive credit and their name on the cover of the book, in a smaller font, underneath the celebrity's name. Others may only be thanked in the acknowledgments section, foregoing a byline.

2. THE BOOK PROPOSAL WILL COME FIRST WHEN THE BOOK IS NONFICTION, AND THE WRITER IS A PROVEN WRITER WITH A PROVEN AUDIENCE.

There is a big difference between long-form content and short-form content. Sometimes new writers think that because they have regularly written blog posts (1,500 words) or magazine articles (2,500 words), they would be able to write a book (50,000 words), but publishers know that this is not always the case. So if a writer has shown proficiency because they already have written and published books, then they can submit a book proposal first. The agent and publisher both believe that the writer will be able to deliver the manuscript on time.

If that writer also has a proven audience, meaning that they have a social media following or email list of people who are accustomed to buying (something, anything) from them, then they also can submit the book proposal first. A proven audience of buyers will not be difficult to move toward purchasing again … namely, a new book.

In both cases, one of the reasons that publishers like the opportunity to receive a book proposal before the manuscript is written is because they like having some input, as far as content. As you will read in the upcoming chapter about traditional publishing, they are motivated by their own best interests, as well as the best interests of the author.

A BOOK PROPOSAL IS JUST A MATCHING DOLLHOUSE, THE MINIATURE VERSION OF YOUR MANUSCRIPT.

If you are reading this book, my guess is that it is because you do not fit into the two previous categories, or you would have already moved forward. Therefore, you will likely need to write your book proposal after you finish the manuscript. In the case of both of my traditionally published books, I wrote the book proposal after I finished the manuscript. Let's quickly make the decision that this is what you will do, too. No need to spend precious time in deliberation. You will pattern the miniature after the original. This will serve you well, no matter your path to publication.

What follows are the components of a book proposal and why each component is necessary. If you would like to access my book proposal walk-through video and template in order to follow along while you read, please go to www.nikamaples.com/bookproposal to download these resources.

1. COVER PAGE:

Like any cover page for a document, this page will have the basic information for your project and you. This basic information includes: main title, subtitle, your name, your physical address, your email address, and your phone number. Your header and footer will begin on the next page.

2. OVERVIEW SECTION:

This section provides everything a publisher needs to know if they only have time to glance at one page. It includes basic information about your book, including the title and subtitle, your name and info, and genre. Here is the manuscript status, including number of chapters, word count, and features, such as illustrations or photographs. Also, this is where you will include content summaries: a one-sentence summary, a one-paragraph summary, and a half-page summary.

3. TARGET MARKET SECTION:

Your target market is the group most likely to purchase the book. Now do you see why we spent so much time exploring your ideal reader? In the target market section, you will include a simple description of the audience (your ideal reader) for the book, as well as their characteristics. An important part of this section is your audience's motivations—why they would be looking for a book like this in the first place. Then you will explain their affinity groups—the places they are gathering, either online or in-person. The last item in this section is the reader takeaway. This is The Promise Bridge that you have worked so hard to create. It is the result, what your reader will know or be able to do after they turn the final page. You may experience some feelings of frustration while you complete this section because you think you can't be sure about these details. This is not absolute science. There are no right or wrong answers. It's okay, just make your best guess.

4. THE TABLE OF CONTENTS SECTION:

The chapters of the book (with their titles, if they have them) should be listed here, including any parts or sections.

5. THE CHAPTER SUMMARIES SECTION:

This is where a book proposal's beastly reputation comes from. It is challenging to write a summary for every chapter in your book. These summaries should be less than 150 words, and should adequately describe the progression of the book and what differentiates each chapter from the next. If you have 20 chapters in your book, you will need to write 20, 150-word chapter summaries. That would be about 3,000 words. However, these 3,000 words will require tremendous focus so that you do not sound repetitive or boring. The literary agent or publisher who reads your chapter summaries section should feel as if they have just read the entire book in 2x playback speed.

6. THE AUTHOR SECTION:

All of us are familiar with creating a social media profile. The author section of your book proposal is the closest thing to a profile. It is also your resume, and should include some achievements and experience, as well as basic information and a professional photograph. Beyond your applicable career and education details, add hyperlinks to speech samples and past or upcoming events, books, articles, blogs, or podcasts episodes—both from your own podcast or those on which you have been featured as a guest.

7. THE PLATFORM AND PROMOTION SECTION:

You will list several potential promotion ideas you have in the marketing plan area. This is not about the creative marketing ideas you can imagine, but those you are willing to pursue. Then, you will include your numbers for podcast downloads, email subscribers, and followers of your various social media accounts. Finally, list the people who might agree to endorse your book, and be sure to add their audience description and size beside their name. If you do not have a big audience, it helps to know someone who does.

8. THE COMPARABLE WORKS SECTION:

Do some research to find five books that are similar to yours, and feature them here. You will present front cover images of the books, as well as basic information about the books. But most importantly, you will write a 150-word discussion on what makes your book the same and different from each one. I've seen some writers become discouraged when they get to this point in the book proposal. They think it means that their book won't have a chance if there are already five books that are similar out there in print. This is not what the comparable works section proves; in fact, it is quite the opposite. When there are comparable works selling well, it is proof of concept. It means that there is a proven market for that topic, and your book will likely sell well, too. On the other hand, if you were not able to find a single book on the market that is anything like yours, that may or may not be a good thing. It might mean that your topic is not salable, and a literary agent or publisher will not be interested.

9. THE WRITING SAMPLE SECTION:

The final section of a book proposal will contain three completely finished chapters from the book. They do not have to be three consecutive chapters. It doesn't matter if they come from the middle or end of the book, however, it is a good idea to include Chapter 1. You will need to capture attention with your book proposal in the same way that you capture it in the book itself … with the very first chapter.

Whew! It is quite a task to write a book proposal, and after you are finished, you will know your book inside and out. If you feel exhausted just thinking about this part of the process, encourage your soul with Colossians 3:23-24 which reminds us, "Whatever you do, work at it with all your heart, as working for the Lord, not for human masters, since you know that you will receive an inheritance from the Lord as a reward. It is the Lord Christ you are serving."

This book proposal is an act of worship that you are offering to the King. He sees your effort and is honored.

Please remember that agents and publishers read thousands of book proposals every year. So don't skimp on any details. A completed book proposal may be more than 60 pages, but it is truly the dollhouse version of your manuscript. When industry professionals read through it, they will feel as if they have just been inside the real thing.

Do your best to make their visit delightful.

20

WORK WITH YOUR LITERARY AGENT

I WOULD NOT HAVE SURVIVED living in Bangkok, Thailand without my friend, Joy. Well, perhaps I would have survived, but I certainly would not have been as successful.

I had moved there to be a school teacher to the eight children of three missionary families, and from the beginning, we all knew it was going to be a temporary assignment. I committed to one year. That meant I was not going to attempt to learn the Thai language beyond basic phrases. If I had been living in France or Mexico for a year, I probably would have come home as a fluent speaker of French or Spanish.

But Thai is not the same. It is known to be one of the most difficult languages to learn because it is a tonal language. The same word, uttered with different tones, can have different meanings.

That happened to me when my mother came to Bangkok to visit me for a couple of weeks. My Thai friends could not help laughing when I brought her to church to meet them. When I asked them what I had done wrong, they told me I had used the wrong tone when I said, "I would like you to meet my mother," in Thai, and I had accidentally introduced her as my *dog*.

The missionaries knew I needed support, both because I could not speak the language and because disability made it impossible for me to hop on one of the inexpensive motorcycle taxis and ride "side saddle" the way others did. When I wanted to go somewhere, a friend had to call an actual car taxi service and give the dispatcher the complicated directions to where I was living, above the church. Then, when the car arrived, someone would have to lean in the window and tell the driver where I wanted to go.

It was an inconvenient process, but more than that, it left me vulnerable. Several times, I could not do anything when we veered off the familiar route to the grocery store or mall. I was literally "being taken for a ride," to increase my taxi fare, simply because I could not communicate.

WHEN YOU ARE ENTERING BRAND NEW TERRITORY, YOU CANNOT OVERSTATE THE VALUE OF AN EXPERIENCED GUIDE.

Enter Joy.

Joy was a teenage girl from our church who agreed to run errands for me after school, twice a week. The hourly fee I paid her was nothing compared to the value that she offered me. My whole world opened up when I met her. She truly lived up to her name.

Before Joy, I was falling deeper and deeper into the haze of culture shock. I felt isolated and restricted. With Joy, I was free again. Sometimes, I gave her a list and money, and she went to the grocery store or office supply store for me. I watched from the upstairs window, as she would zip away on the motorcycle taxi, and return the same way, bags hanging from her arms. Other times, she would call for a car taxi, and we would go somewhere together so she could translate for me. One of our favorite spots was the fabric store at the mall. There was a sewing machine at the church so I filled all of my spare time (and there was a lot of it, being that I had so few friends and no television) with sewing projects for the kids in my kindergarten and first grade class. For Mother's Day, I made all three mothers and their daughters matching sundresses, a feat I could never have accomplished if Joy had not been at the fabric store to tell the clerk the measurements of the fabric and the kind of sewing notions I needed.

Joy knew how to get around in the big city. She and I visited interesting restaurants downtown, went to a George Winston piano concert at a university, and enjoyed a weekend at Hua Hin Beach. I could not have done any of those things without her. And she could not have done any of those things without me.

At 16 years of age, she would not have had enough money for any of those experiences. But because she had the language, and I had the means, we were a great team. Her knowledge was not the only thing that was valuable, however. Her understanding was worth much more.

As a native Thai, she understood the culture.

I knew the basics, like the nonnegotiable practice of taking my shoes off at the front door of every home. But I did not know that the bottoms of my feet could not show at all. That's tricky when so many places do not have furniture, and you are expected to sit on the floor. The first time I sat against the wall with my legs out in front of me, Joy scrambled over to me in horror. She whispered that I was making a big mistake and showed me how to twist my legs in such a way that my feet were tightly tucked under my backside. Ordinary cross-legged sitting was completely off-limits because the bottoms of your feet show on either side.

One day, I patted a young man on the head, and he turned to me with daggers in his eyes. Joy quickly intervened and explained to him that I was a *farang*, an expat who didn't know the rules. Later, she warned me never to do that again. Touching the top of someone's head was a tremendous faux pas.

Now you can see why I said I would not have been successful in Bangkok without Joy. When you are entering brand new territory, you cannot overstate the value of an experienced guide.

Enter your literary agent.

If you have decided to pursue traditional publication, you must have a literary agent to represent you and your project. In this chapter, I will tell you why you need one, how to get one, and what it looks like to work with one.

WHY YOU NEED A LITERARY AGENT:

No matter what you think you already know about the culture and practices of the publishing industry, you don't know enough. Just accept it. Like my time in Bangkok, you know enough to take your shoes off at the door, but you don't know the rules once you are inside. There are nuances to publishing that only those who have been in the industry for decades can navigate with ease. Trust me, you need a guide.

1. A LITERARY AGENT IS THE ONLY WAY TO GET TO A PUBLISHER. Many years ago, a new writer could actually send a manuscript directly to a publishing house. In fact, they could send a hard copy. That is what I did with my first book. These days, the standard practice is to approach the publishing house via a literary agent. That literary agent will not be using a hard copy of your manuscript when they do it, either. They will be relying upon your book proposal to communicate with acquisitions editors.

You might be saying, "But what if I know someone who works for a traditional publisher? Do I still have to go through a literary agent?"

Well, I suppose there are some instances where current day authors have not worked with a literary agent, but when it is such a rare occurence, why would you even want to spend any time thinking about it? The chances of this happening are slim to none. Besides, if you were somehow able to get the attention of a publisher without the help of an agent, they would eventually send you to get an agent anyway.

2. A LITERARY AGENT HAS CONNECTIONS. The publishing world looks enormous from the outside, but you would be surprised how small it is. Everyone seems to know one another. And if they haven't formally worked together, yet, they know the friend of a friend who used to work with them, and it is only a matter of time until they meet. Industry professionals switch publishing houses, as well as positions within those houses, and so you never know who someone knows. You just have to assume that everyone knows everyone.

Your literary agent will know which publisher and acquisitions editor is likely to want your manuscript. They will know that a certain editor prefers a certain style of writing or is looking for a certain type of book. Those connections work in your favor and make a publishing contract happen faster. Trust has already been established between the agent and the editor, or they are willing to trust, based on mutual respect.

3. A LITERARY AGENT NEGOTIATES BETTER. Once I heard of a publisher who offered a now well-known Christian author a book contract back when she was only a blogger. The deal was for an advance of $5,000. Then she reached out to a literary agent and secured her representation. A few conversations later, and the same publisher offered her an advance of $15,000.

An author's **advance** is the amount of money that a traditional publishing house offers to the writer in exchange for the exclusive printing rights of the book. But money is not the only point of negotiation in a contract. You will want to come to favorable terms regarding everything about the book, from the audio recording to percentage of royalties to what happens if it doesn't sell well. These are tedious details that have long-term effects. You do not want to skim over them. A literary agent has the expertise you need in order to feel secure and confident about the deal you are making.

4. A LITERARY AGENT IS YOUR ADVOCATE. You cannot predict what may or may not happen during your publication journey. During the tense months before your book's release, as well as the years following, you want someone who will serve as a buffer between you and your publisher. Your agent will fight for you and your book's success, sometimes saying things that you cannot say and always drawing both parties back to the fine print of the contract.

HOW TO GET A LITERARY AGENT:

There is not a formula for you to follow when looking for a literary agent. There are several ways to go about it.

You might meet your literary agent at a conference for writers. Many of these types of conferences allow you to add-on a 15-minute appointment with a literary agent for an extra fee. It's typical that you won't get to choose a particular agent; you will just be paired with one based upon when you enrolled and how many spots are available. During your brief appointment, you will need to be prepared. Bring your book proposal, in case the agent wants to take it immediately. More than likely, they will ask you to email them a copy of the proposal if they are interested. Also bring along a one-pager, similar to the author section in your book proposal, that has a clear list of your personal information and professional qualifications. Always include a photograph. Before you go, practice pitching your book until it feels natural and simple to do so.

You might meet your literary agent through a referral, like I did. A talent agent at the speaker's bureau that represents me suggested that I work with a certain literary agent for my next book. The talent agent made an email introduction, and we took it from there. The literary agent was not interested in my initial book proposal, but he did believe I had potential as an author. He and I worked together on a new book proposal for months, and he offered a contract to represent me, one year after our email introduction.

You might meet your literary agent through your own research. If you can name a couple of authors with writing similar to yours, scour their acknowledgments page for their literary agent. Most authors mention this. Then go to the literary agent's website. They might work for a bigger agency with several agents, and they might have their own agency under their name. Be diligent. You will find them. Then study their submissions guidelines and follow them to the letter. Every agent is different so do not assume that you can approach them all the same way. In fact, some request that you not pitch them at the same time that you pitch another agent. Be respectful of this request. If you want them to pay attention to details when they study your book contract, you must show them that you can pay attention to details when you study their submissions guidelines.

You might meet your literary agent when you look through a web site with a current list of literary agents. When you find one that interests you, follow their submission guidelines, as stated above.

Keep in mind that literary agents are inundated with thousands of queries every year. They do not owe you a rejection letter, and many will not respond when they are not interested in your proposal. So if it has been about two months, and you still have not heard anything from the agents you have queried, then simply move on to the next batch. Do *not* contact them to ask if they received your query.

WHAT IT LOOKS LIKE TO WORK WITH A LITERARY AGENT:

When you have signed a contract to work with a literary agent, and they have agreed to pitch your proposal to publishers, then you just wait. They will be in touch when there are updates. In between nibbles and bites from publishers, there will be silence, kind of like when you go fishing on a pond. Everything is happening under the surface.

And then something finally comes up, and the agent will ask you if you are interested in the offer made by a particular publisher. If you are, the agent will introduce you to the acquisitions editor, and the ball will start rolling.

From the contract to the bookshelf, throughout the entire process, your agent will be copied on emails and available for questions. And why are they so present and interested in the book?

Because your success is their success. By engaging with a literary agent, you agree to give them a cut of the advance and royalties for the life of the book. With every literary agent, the percentage will be different but for most, it is around 15%.

That may seem like a lot, but their knowledge and understanding of the publishing culture is well worth it.

They are fluent in a language you don't speak.

21

JOIN YOUR PUBLISHING TEAM

THE LOWEST MOMENT IN MY WRITING career is painful to think about. Years ago, an acquaintance of an acquaintance of an acquaintance had read some of my earliest blog posts and believed that I would one day be a successful author. That person knew I needed connections wherever I could find them. And he arranged a telephone meeting between me and someone who had held a significant role in the publishing industry for decades. He was hoping I could ask some questions and receive helpful advice.

I remember waiting for that phone call with rocks in my stomach. I believed this was my big break, the moment I had dreamed of my whole life. Nothing could go wrong; I had practiced every word I would say.

The moment arrived, and the industry professional and I spoke for a total of twenty minutes. The whole time, I felt like I was a kid on the playground, trying to convince him to pick me for the team. I was afraid this was my only chance.

For a few moments toward the end of the conversation, I had a feeling things were going well, and I started to relax.

Then the professional abruptly changed his tone and asked one question that is forever burned in my memory, not because of his words, but because of my answer to them.

"Nika, do you know what a big deal it is for someone like you to be talking to someone like me?" he said. The question was loaded. A power move. He knew he held all the cards.

Then timidly, nervously, desperately, I answered: "Yes."

I cringe as I relive the memory. He had suggested that he was more important than I was. And I agreed with him.

Of all the failures I have weathered over the years, this is my only regret. In that brief second I was given to reply, I had believed I was less-than. For just an instant, I had forgotten that both of us were image-bearers of the Almighty and are equal in His sight. It would be years later before I grew in wisdom, maturity, and God-confidence enough to think differently about his question.

How would I answer *now*?

I wouldn't. I would thank him for his time and end the conversation immediately. Just hearing that question come from someone's mouth would be the neon clue that I don't want to enter a partnership with them. You cannot accomplish meaningful work with someone who thinks they are better than you.

Especially if you agree.

If you are considering traditional publishing for your book, then you need to know there are a lot of gatekeepers you will need to pass through in the process. Not all of them will have the attitude of the person I just described, but even the kindest person in the world can be toxic in your life if you believe you are beholden to them. No one in the traditional publishing world is "doing you a favor." Publishing is a business. You need them, and they need you. Did you hear me? They *need* you. Without your ideas and words, there is no book to publish.

Traditional publishing is a team effort.

So here is a brief primer of what to expect when you join your traditional publishing team.

THE BEGINNING:

Your literary agent will pitch your book proposal to an **acquisitions editor.** If the acquisitions editor selects your manuscript to move forward, they will act as an advocate for you. The next stop is the **editorial board** (ed board) of the publishing house. This group of people will determine whether your topic is relevant and whether the writing itself is the caliber of their other authors. If they select your book proposal to move forward, the next stop is the **publication board** (pub board). This group of people evaluate the business side of publishing your book. They look at your previous accomplishments, the size of your audience on social media, your experience with presenting and interviewing, and determine the general saleability of your book. It doesn't matter how beautiful your writing is if they can't sell it.

When you make it through the acquisitions editor, ed board, and pub board, and the publisher has decided to make you an offer, your literary agent will contact you to let you know that negotiations have begun on a book contract. This is why you need an agent. They take care of everything at this stage, thankfully. Your agent will explain every detail of the contract before you sign.

When you enter into the contract, you agree to an **advance** in exchange for the printing rights to your book. An advance is an amount of money that the publisher pays you before the book is created. I kind of think of it as a loan that you don't have to pay back. If the publisher pays you an advance of $30,000, you will not ever owe that money back to them (unless you do not deliver the manuscript as promised), however, you will not make another dime until you "sell-through" the advance. That means every book sale counts against the advance until you reach $30,000.01. After that first cent over the advance, you will receive **royalties** from all future book sales. Be aware that it is harder to sell-through an advance than you think, and most authors never do.

It is important to note that the advance is not distributed in one lump sum. It is broken down into smaller chunks that are attached to certain milestones in the publishing process. You may get $4,500 for signing the contract, then $5,500 for turning in the manuscript, then $3,000 for turning in your marketing plan, and so on, until the final installment on the day of the book's release. This is important to know because it can be 18 to 24 months between the signed contract and the book's release. An advance of $30,000 sounds incredible when you fantasize that it will arrive in one lump sum. But it loses its shine when you realize it will arrive in bits and pieces over a two-year period. Think of it as working a job for which you are paid $15,000 annually. That's below the poverty line. Not many people explain this before you enter the traditional publishing world, but I think it is important to know *how* as well as *what* you will be compensated.

There are a few other enlightening details you should know about how you will be compensated in a traditional publishing agreement. As I stated, your book sales will count against the advance, and when you sell-through, you will begin earning royalties. But as you do the calculations to determine how fast you could sell-through, please do not think in terms of the retail price of the book. If you did that with a book priced at $15.99, you might think you only have to sell 1,876 books in order to sell-through. But that is not the case.

YOUR LITERARY AGENT IS THERE TO HELP YOU THROUGH THE WEEDS.

Other entities take the lion's share of the sale. The bookstore or online retailer gets their cut. Then the publisher gets their cut, which includes the expense of producing the book (paying editors, designers, and sales team members) and printing the book (paper, ink, glue, shipping, and warehousing). Most authors retain only 16% of the sale.

That check (as well as all of the checks that comprise the author advance) goes to your literary agent, not to you. The literary agent then takes a 15% cut, and you will finally receive your check from your agent ... which is 85% of 16% of the sale of your $15.99 book. Also, it arrives 90 days after you meet the milestone written into the contract.

In other words, it will take a lot more books to sell-through your advance than you think. The entire retail price does not count against the sale of the book. Only your 16% does. So at

$2.50 a book, that means you will finally sell-through your $30,000 advance after 12,000 book sales.

It's gonna be a lot of work before you see your next penny.

And it is worth noting that your contract will have different percentages for different types of books … audio book, e-book, hard cover, paperback, mass market paperback (the kind with unattractive, rough paper), books in other languages, etc. All of these details are why your agent deserves their cut. Your literary agent is there to help you through the weeds.

THE MIDDLE:

The main reason most new authors want to go the traditional publishing route is because they want the publisher to handle all of the production, distribution, and marketing. Two of those are reasonable expectations to have of your traditional publisher, one is not.

Your traditional publishing team is a powerhouse when it comes to production and distribution. They will have a first-class team of editors (developmental editors, copy editors, and proofreaders) on the project to make your book as flawless as possible. You will have some interactions with these team members, but there will be long periods of silence, as well. You won't hear from anyone for weeks, and then an edited manuscript will be sent to you for review. You must read the entire thing, and then you will be allowed minimal pushback in areas where you question the edits.

Your traditional publisher will also have an interior designer typesetting your words to make them readable and beautiful on the page. When the text is typeset, you will receive **galley proofs** (usually digitally). Galley proofs will show you what your book will look like in print. You will be invited to read through the galley proofs one more time before the book goes to print. Seeing the galleys for the first time is my favorite moment. Your manuscript will really look like a book for the first time. There is nothing so important as a stunning interior.

The cover designer will create a fantastic cover that will meet market standards and compete with other titles in your genre. (Sometimes you will have some input in the cover design, but other times you won't. For *Hunting Hope*, I was invited to come to the office and view a selection of five possible covers. We all discussed which one was right for the book. In the case of *Everyday Genesis*, I was not given a choice. Only one cover was sent to me, but I loved it instantly so it wasn't a problem that I didn't have a choice. The cover design is often one of the first things decided (sometimes, even before the manuscript is turned in) because it will be used in promotional materials and posted for pre-orders online.

THE END:
After your book is created, a traditional publisher can print them at a remarkable discount because they are printing so many books at one time. They have an advantage in this regard.

A sales team will do their best to distribute your book in as many places as possible. Be forewarned that just having a traditionally-published book does not mean you will be in every store or airport. The sales team will be selling your book to these outlets, and some will agree to carry your book, but some won't. The connections that a sales team can make is one of the big reasons to choose traditional publishing.

But marketing is not a reason at all. Your traditional publisher will do very little to market your book. Their promotional budgets are reserved for celebrity authors who have an enormous readership champing at the bit to buy their next title.

Everybody else has to do their own marketing.

Oh, there will be a few things a traditional publisher might do for you in the first 90 days of a book's release, like help you land interviews on a few radio shows, but even so, the majority of the marketing is up to you.

In fact, it was a real shock to me to find out that one of the compensation milestones in a book contract is your marketing plan. You will need to turn in a detailed plan to market and sell your book. This task is tied to one of the payments of your advance. You may want to outsource the creation of this marketing plan and work with someone who will help you outline the promotions you need to make sales. I did this for both of my traditionally-published books.

On that wonderful Tuesday when your book launches (Books always release on Tuesdays), you will feel ready to conquer the world. Launch day is truly a glorious day. But the work has only just begun. And what if your books do not sell as well as you hope? Well, there are a few things I think you should know.

You have sold your printing rights. Not your copyright; that's still yours. But your printing rights are not. So if you want to boost your book sales by creating ancillary works like a group Bible study that goes with the book or notecards or a calendar with quotations, you will have to discuss it with your literary agent. Depending on your contract, some of these ideas are not available to you.

And there is another thing. Printing the actual book is not available to you, even if your publisher decides to stop printing it, like they did with me. *Everyday Genesis* did not sell as well as we hoped, even though it is one of my favorite books I've ever written. The poor sales were entirely due to the fact that I did not not market the book. It is very much my fault.

But three years after it was released, the publisher decided to stop printing it and still had copies in the warehouse that they were going to destroy or sell to markdown outlets. So they called me to ask if I wanted to buy the books before they liquidated them.

I said yes, yes, yes!

I could not stand the thought of something I had created meeting an untimely end. So I made personal sacrifices and took money out of my retirement account to buy them back. Now they are stored in a small warehouse near where I live. We sell them in my online shop and ship them from the warehouse. But I still cannot print any new copies because I don't own my own printing rights. One day, I will buy the rights back from the publisher and begin printing the books again.

You see, I love my own creation so much that I am willing to do anything to redeem it from destruction and empower it to fulfill its purpose.

Sounds familiar, doesn't it?

22

EXPAND YOUR SELF-PUBLISHING

EVERYTHING CHANGED WHEN I LOOKED over my mother's shoulder. She was reading the newspaper, and noticed something I had never paid attention to before.

The ads.

"Why do some companies get to have pictures in the paper?"

She explained that they had paid a fee for different sizes of space.

"You mean all you have to do is start a newspaper, and people will pay to be on your pages? They'll pay you *real* money?"

She nodded.

That was when I learned you could actually create income by publishing, and I knew I'd never do anything else.

I was ten years old when I self-published *The Maples Messenger*, a monthly family newsletter. It was 1983, so creating a newsletter meant that I would type articles on my typewriter and later, cut and paste them together with real scissors and tape. It took me weeks to write and design each issue. Then my mother would make copies for me, and I would fold, address, and put a stamp on each one.

Writing has always been my happy place, and the newsletter kept me delightfully busy. Instead of watching TV, I would bang out articles, op-eds, prayer requests (listed, church-bulletin style), jokes, and announcements after school until mom called us to dinner. It should come as no surprise that my favorite part was the advertising section. The ads were the whole reason I had started *The Maples Messenger* in the first place.

The same day that my mother had explained the concept of advertising, I had run to my room to write out my elementary business plan. After some thought, I determined that I could sell newsletter subscriptions for a dollar a month, and advertising space for five dollars a month.

YOU ARE INVESTING IN THE KINGDOM WHEN YOU INVEST IN A KID.

A handful of family and friends subscribed. But in the end, only one person purchased ads. My mom's lifelong friend, Dr. Hill, is an inventor and accomplished scientist, and he paid for both a subscription *and* ad space, sending me six whole dollars in the mail at the beginning of every month.

I was a *millionaire*.

Why would a shrewd businessman in New Jersey take the time to put six dollars and ad copy in an envelope and send it to an ambitious third grader in Texas every month? There was no ROI for him; the circulation of my newsletter was less than a dozen. Yet, in my mind's eye, I can see him picking up the phone when I had called to pitch the newsletter. It's easy to imagine a wide grin spreading across his face, as a ten-year-old asked him if he would like to buy in. His entrepreneurial heart must have recognized the eager voice of a dreamer.

And so my first-and-only advertiser said yes, and just like that, my lifelong passion and divine assignment came into view.

You are investing in the Kingdom when you invest in a kid.

Just like it was when I was just a child on "typewriter training wheels," self-publishing is still a lucrative option for anyone who is willing to work diligently. Years ago, there was a stigma to it, as people esteemed an author more if their work had been selected by the "gatekeepers" of literary agents and traditional publishing houses. But somewhere along the way, three things happened. One, self-publishing options improved dramatically. Two, the birth of the Internet made it possible to market and distribute widely. And three, people just got tired of gatekeepers making all the decisions.

As you know, several of my books are self-published. So why would anyone choose self-publishing over traditional publishing?

SELF-PUBLISHING IS FASTER.
You can get a book into readers' hands at a remarkable speed. There is really no limit. It all depends on how fast you and your contractors can work together.

SELF-PUBLISHING HAS A HIGHER ROI (RETURN ON INVESTMENT).
When both a literary agent and a publisher are taking a cut of your advance and royalties, that doesn't leave you with much. If you are willing to forego the big financial boon on the front end and save it for the back end, there is an opportunity to make a lot more money.

SELF-PUBLISHING IS FREEDOM.
You choose the content. You choose the formatting and size. You choose the cover. You choose the release date. You choose the retail price. You choose. You choose. You choose.

And, you get to respond directly to what your audience wants. For instance, when I pitched *Keep Teaching* to my literary agent and publisher, they didn't think there was a big enough audience for devotional books for educators. I knew otherwise. I had been a teacher myself and had spoken to countless teachers across the nation in my travels as Texas Secondary Teacher of the Year. I knew people would love it.

So when no publisher wanted it, I self-published. And that book has sold more than all of my others combined, including my traditionally-published titles.

Here is my advice if you self-publish:

HIRE AN EDITOR. I have already explained why this is important. Good editors may charge a flat fee for the project or charge by the word. Check online for current prices before you sign a contract. It really depends on the length of your book, but a general guideline is $1,000-4,000.

HIRE A BOOK DESIGNER. Please do not try to do this yourself. Your artist friend is not the best choice, either. There are important design principles for both the cover and interior that are specific to a book, and the software required to typeset a book is far too complex to learn on a whim. A novice would never be able to create a professional book. A full manuscript is a massive amount of text so it's best to call in the experts. I can spot books created on Microsoft Word from 50 yards. You will never be sorry you paid a designer.

HAVE YOUR BOOK COMPONENTS READY TO GIVE THE INTERIOR AND COVER DESIGNER: The body of the work is not the only thing you will need.

1. CREATE A DESIGN BRIEF. Your designer will want to know what kind of branding you desire for your book. They are not going to read the whole thing and come up with a concept on their own. They will want to see five book covers that you like and five that you don't. Write a few sentences, explaining why you feel that way. Suggest colors or images you think would work well.

Use Amazon or GoodReads (www.goodreads.com) as a search tool for this. Type in your proposed title and/or subtitle. Is it already taken? How long ago was it published? How many reviews does it have? Just because a title is taken doesn't mean you can't use it. But if it was recently published or has a wide readership with lots of reviews, you probably don't want to compete. It isn't worth it. What do other books in your category look like? Are all of the covers similar? How can you stand out? Take note that the most compelling book covers are clear even in the thumbnail image. So don't overcomplicate the ideas for your design. Keep it clean.

Your book designer will probably give you four revisions for both the cover and the interior. I've always picked the first interior they sent me. But with the cover, I've taken all four revisions.

This is what it looks like. Your designer will create about five designs that are very different and send them to you. If you like none of them and want them to send you an entirely new set of five, that will be your first revision. Otherwise, you will pick a favorite and move forward.

Then they will recreate that one favorite five different ways, meaning they will use different fonts or change small details in the design. That is a revision (either first or second, as the case may be).

You will pick a favorite from that revised group and keep suggesting small changes until you are satisfied or you hit your fourth revision. The reason there is a practice of limiting revisions is to avoid what is known as "scope creep." Designers have project calendars, and then are balancing your project among many others. They cannot go on and on with an indecisive author. However, if a few more changes need to be made, the designer will usually agree, as long as you pay an additional fee for the extended work.

Good designers are one of the best expenses you will pay to create your book. I hired the same designer who did the cover for my traditionally-published book, *Everyday Genesis*, to design three more books for me. Why? Because over and over again, people have told me that they picked up *Everyday Genesis* on a whim because they loved its cover, even though they had never heard of me. When people judge a book by its cover, why wouldn't you prioritize paying for a good designer? A general guideline is $2,000-4,000 for a combined package of both interior and cover.

2. WRITE YOUR DUST JACKET COPY. Your **dust jacket copy** is important because it will be used in so many ways. It may be used in your query letter to your agent. It may be used in your book proposal. Most of all, it will be used to attract your reader and let them know that your book is for them. I am using the term "dust jacket copy" loosely here. **Copy** is a word

that means convincing or persuasive language when it comes to marketing a book. **Dust jacket** refers to anything on the outside of the book, not on actual pages. So you may have a hardcover book with a paper wrapper around it. In that case, the dust jacket includes the inside flaps in the front and back. But it also includes the back cover copy. Paperback books will usually only have only the back copy, unless they are a paperback book with **French folds**. French folds are the flaps that extend the front and back cover and fold inside a paperback book.

There was a time when having a book printed in hard cover with a dust jacket signified that it was more legitimate. That is no longer the case. Now a high quality paperback book is all that is needed to bolster your career and give you greater authority. No matter the type of book you are creating, it is important to write compelling dust jacket copy that would make any reader buy the book. This includes information about why the reader should want to read the book, as well as your author bio and professional author photo.

3. OBTAIN YOUR ISBN AND BARCODE. Your **ISBN** is your International Standard Book Number, and it differentiates your book from any other book, even with the same title. It is a ten or 13-digit number that you register with Bowker Identifier Services found at www.myidentifiers.com. You can purchase one ISBN or a block of ISBNs for future use. When you register the ISBN, you will need basic information, including your dust jacket copy and author bio. Your ISBN will be associated with a barcode, which you can also purchase with Bowker. Your designer will want to put it on the back cover of your book. Plenty of videos on YouTube will walk you through obtaining your ISBN and barcode with Bowker.

4. COMPLETE YOUR FRONT AND BACK MATTER. The **front and back matter** of your book are all of the things that go before and after your manuscript. Front matter includes: the copyright page, testimonials and reviews, the first and second title pages, the dedication page, etc. Back matter includes: the index, the appendix, acknowledgments, an extended author bio, and any advertisements for your web site or other books. A self-published author can have more control

about whether to include advertisements, especially if they are printing on demand, which I will explain in the next section.

CHOOSE YOUR TYPE OF PRINTING. The cover designer will deliver a PDF of your cover spread, as if you were looking at your book opened wide, with both the front cover and back cover showing at the same time. They will have used a precise spine calculation to determine the exact measurements, based on the number of pages in your book and the width of the paper you have chosen. It is a specific process that is one more reason I insist that you use a designer instead of trying to create a book cover yourself. The interior designer will deliver a PDF of your interior pages, in a single, page-by-page view.

Now you need to decide how you will print your books. There are three ways.

1. OFFSET PRINTING. This is a form of printing that provides high-volume printing for the lowest price per book but the highest expense upfront. An offset printer will create giant metal plates from your PDFs of the cover and interior, and they will print your books by loading the ink onto the metal plates and running paper through a printing press. With offset printing, typos and mistakes are costly. The metal plate must be recreated, even to fix one letter. And if you have already printed 5,000 books, then all of those books will still have the mistake in them, even if future books do not. When books are printed this way, they must be stored in a garage or warehouse and shipped when purchased. One of the dangers is that the longer the books wait to be sold, the more chances there are that they will be damaged by accidents, temperature, insects, or passing time. Offset printers will only print large print runs at a time, so it is a significant investment to go this route. Also, there is the additional detail of having page numbers in multiples of 16. Offset printers use paper that has been folded into sixteen sheets, called **signatures**. That means you may need to include advertisements if you have some blank pages at the end. Or you may not be able to include advertisements, if there are not enough pages left in the signature. If you choose to work with an offset printer, I recommend Bass Printing (www.bassprintingw2p.com). They are highly experienced and helpful. Owned

by Christians; located in Fort Worth, Texas. They ship anywhere.

2. DIGITAL PRINTING. If you choose a digital printer, you have a lot more control, but you pay more per book. The price to offset print a book might be $1.50 while the price to digitally print a book might be $7.50. The advantages are that there is no minimum print run. So you can print a small amount of books for a few hundred dollars instead of a large amount of books for tens of thousands of dollars. Digital printing does not require metal plates to be created because it works more like a large computer printer, rather than a printing press with ink. Therefore, making a change or correcting a mistake comes at very little cost and almost no additional time. A digital printer is not tied to a specific number of pages per book, either. You do not have to work in multiples of 16. You will still have to store and ship the books, but you won't have to store as many.

Offset printing offers ink that is slightly more durable than digital printing. It is possible that the colors may have slight variations and, on very rare occassions, may smudge with digital printing. But most readers will never be able to tell the difference between a book that is digitally printed and one that is offset printed. The quality of digital printers is fantastic. I use them all the time. In fact, if you choose to work with a digital printer, I recommend Trinity Digital Printing (www.trinitydigitalprinting.com). They are highly experienced and helpful. Owned by Christians; located in Fort Worth, Texas. They ship anywhere.

Finally, if you choose either one of these printing options, please avoid storing your books in your garage. Inevitably, they will be damaged, and you will grow to hate them. Treat yourself like a professional and invest in warehousing. If you are looking for a distributor with warehousing space to store your books and systems to take your orders and ship them with ease, I recommend Sweet Distributors (www.sweetdistributors.com). They are highly experienced and helpful. Owned by Christians; located in Fort Worth, Texas. They receive from and ship to anywhere.

3. PRINT ON DEMAND. Known as POD, this is by far the easiest way to self-publish, although it has the smallest profit margin. When a book is **print on demand**, it doesn't exist until a consumer clicks the purchase button. When that happens, the wheels go into motion immediately, and a book is printed and sent directly to the reader. There are no warehousing or shipping concerns for the author. The sales tax and shipping costs are incurred by the online retailer, which is such a relief. The online retailer also gets a cut of the sale, which means the author gets even less than if they had chosen digital printing, but there might be even more sales because online retailers are search engines in and of themselves and can bring in some readers that wouldn't have found you any other way. If you choose to work with a print-on-demand printer, I recommend Ingram Spark at www.ingramspark.com. You will be able to find many up-to-date instructional videos to walk you through the process of uploading your first book. The moment you do, it will be available on Amazon and most major online retailers. You will be compensated for book sales every 90 days.

The freedom available for a self-published author is outstanding. As long as you are willing to take on expenses on the front end, as well as the responsibility of project management, you stand to create more income on the back end. And if you are anything like me, you will cherish the choice that comes with self-publishing. I am hesitant to give up the control over design and content now that I have learned how to make it work so well.

But in order to be a self-published author, you are going to have to develop a powerful ability to choose more than just production elements.

You are going to have to learn to choose *yourself*.

There are no gatekeepers to tell you if your book is good enough. You have to be the one to take the risk and allow readers to respond to it before you feel ready. With the right perspective, that won't be difficult. Think of it this way: when you became a Christian, you committed to following Jesus, right?

Well, the Bible says that He was the first One to choose you. So if you are really going to follow in His footsteps, you know what that means ...

Download your workbook at
www.nikamaples.com/popd_workbook

STEP FIVE

Marketing & Selling

She perceives that her merchandise is profitable. Her lamp does not go out at night.

Proverbs 31:18 ESV

23

LAUNCH YOUR BOOK

WHEN THE GUESTS WALKED INTO the small chapel, the foyer was empty. No decorations, no food, no flowers. I had created a brief presentation for the launch party for *Hunting Hope*, and all of it was going to take about 45 minutes. A friend of mine sang a song and played guitar, then there was a slideshow, and finally, I spoke for about 30 minutes on the power of hope.

The doors of the chapel were closed when the last guest arrived. Then my team got to work, transforming the foyer into something truly special.

We had spent weeks creating a backdrop of streamers, attached to a rope and pulley system, so that my team could lower a massive curtain of streamers from the balcony overhead. They rolled out trays and tables of all kinds of food, along with huge vases of flowers. We even had a keyboard with a classical pianist who was poised to start playing on cue.

When I said the final line of my speech, the back doors of the chapel opened simultaneously, and the guests turned around to see a foyer that had been transformed.

Everyone *oohed* and *ahhed*. My talk had been based upon John 5:17, which reminds us that God is always working, even when we can't see the evidence. Jesus is always working, too. That is our basis for hope. So the perfect illustration of this concept was to have my launch party guests come into the chapel, passing through an empty foyer. Less than an hour later, they excited the chapel to find a wonderland.

That night, people eagerly stood in line for an hour so that I could greet each person and sign their copy of *Hunting Hope*.

I sold 400 books.

You will want to plan the launch of your book in three significant areas, working backward from the launch party:

THE LAUNCH PARTY:
On the night of the book's release or a day or two after, host a party. Mine was at a church, but you can choose any kind of venue. Be creative. Choose something that reflects the topic of your book. Bookstores, libraries, and cafes are great places to start.

You can make your launch party public and invite guests through a social media post, but I would also send out a few invitations through snail mail. You want to make sure you have a good turn out.

I love launch parties that match the book cover, with decorations in a similar color, food and snacks that fit the theme, and music that evokes a certain atmosphere. If your readers were able to smell, touch, taste, hear, and see your book, what would the experience be like?

You can prepare a show of sorts, with a variety of features, but the most important aspect of a book launch is you. Your guests will expect you to give a short speech or to read aloud from the book.

At the party, make sure you have ordered plenty of copies of the book to have on hand. People love a signed copy from the launch party. You will need to set up a way to make transactions and train a couple of people who can handle that side of things for you while you greet your guests. If you are having your event at a bookstore or cafe, they may suggest that the sales go through the register. I usually choose to use a card reader and make transactions right at the book table. A helper will run the transaction and then give the buyer a few sticky notes so that they can write down the names of everyone for whom they want a book signed. If the person wants three books signed, it certainly helps me to focus on smiling and interacting with them while I quickly look at the sticky notes and sign the books to the correct people. It saves me having to interrupt and ask for correct spellings repeatedly.

You can decide if you want the books sold at your launch party to be offered at a discount. I never have done so, but that is entirely up to you. My opinion is that the discounts are best when offered as a pre-order incentive. They are no longer applicable after the book has been released.

THE LAUNCH TEAM:

Your launch team will be instrumental in spreading the word about your book and writing your first reviews online. People like to be part of a book launch team because they are the first ones to read it, and it feels like an exclusive privilege to interact with the author behind the scenes.

In the past, I have done an all-call on social media to ask if anyone wanted to be on my launch team. You would be surprised how many people volunteer, especially if you offer them an incentive, like a chance to join a special online meeting and meet you or ask questions. Or if your launch party is by invitation-only, you could give them an opportunity to come.

As new volunteers express interest, I create a form for people who are interested so I can collect their names, email addresses, and home addresses. Then I send each person on the launch team an ARC, or **advanced reader copy**. You can have these printed with a digital printer and put a sticker on each one that says they are not for sale. You might be tempted to send your launch team digital copies only, but then they won't have the book available to take photos to post on social media! Giving them physical copies is worth the investment.

When you send the book, include a letter to express your gratitude and offer instructions so they know what to expect. Here are some ideas for what to include in their instructions:

1. You could create a private Facebook group for the launch team, where you post images and quotes that they can use in their social media promotions.

2. You could create a posting calendar that they can consult in order to know what to

promote and when.

3. You could give them a checklist of activities, from posting a review at an online retailer to doing an Instagram Live about the book.

4. You could give them an extra copy of the book and tell them to offer it as a giveaway.

5. You could ask them to have you as a guest interview on their podcast, Instagram Live, YouTube video or Facebook Live.

This list is just the beginning of things you could offer as support to your launch team. Most of all, express your gratitude for their willingness to help you promote your book. Their gift of time, effort, and recommendation are worth a great deal.

THE LAUNCH PLAN:
It will take about three to six months of focused effort to launch your book properly. You need to create a long runway for it to be successful in getting off the ground. A long runway means that you need to start pointing people to your book long before it is time to purchase it.

Your blog, podcast, social media, and YouTube channel should all point to the book in subtle ways for weeks. You can prepare for this emphasis by getting a calendar on which you can plan your content up until (and immediately after) the book launch.

As you plan, make sure your content increasingly directs your audience to purchase. The more pre-orders you can generate, the more early reviews you will have online. Pre-orders will come when you offer the book at a pre-order discount and if you offer it with a pre-order package. In the past, my pre-order package included digital offerings like a coloring book with quotes from the book, various phone wallpapers related to the book, and a hard copy of stationery mailed to their home. I still have some of the notecards I created to go with the *Hunting Hope* launch. But one of the best pre-order incentives I ever offered was a digital download of five original songs. One of my friends is a songwriter, and I asked her to write and record five songs, based on the book. We sent the digital files to everyone who pre-ordered the book and could provide proof of purchase.

Pre-orders are so important, that I have a suggestion that may surprise you: One of the things you can consider if you are self-publishing is pre-selling your book before it is written. I know, I know. It sounds scary. But if I could go back and do it all over again, this is the one thing I would change about my writing career.

My very first conference about writing or publishing was called The Mega Book Marketing Seminar, hosted by Mark Victor Hansen, the co-creator of the *Chicken Soup for the Soul* books. I was so afraid to attend the conference and step into my identity as an author, that I actually purchased a second ticket (about $1500 each!) for my brother and paid for his airfare to fly with me from Texas to Florida for the event. We were both surprised to hear so many of the presenters recommend pre-selling your self-published book before you write it.

I thought, *No way! That is too dangerous!*

But over and over again, we would meet people who had done it. They said it provided capital for the printing and was a good gauge for reader interest. It was the ultimate proof of concept. And if you approached it well, you could shape your content by interacting with the early adopters who purchased the book in the pre-sale. I dismissed the idea without even considering it.

It would be twenty years later before I tried it and saw how well it worked. I wish I had followed Hansen's advice long before. The thing about a coach's advice is that it is always going to sound counterintuitive. If it were something you knew to do, you would have already done it. But you hire a coach because you need someone to call a different play than the one you have been using. That's why I wish I could go back and tell myself that hiring a coach who will call a different play is not enough.

You actually have to run it.

FIND YOUR BRAND VOICE

by Anita Albert-Watson

IT IS NOW TIME TO FIND your brand voice. I've found that when most people think about branding, they immediately think about the visual aspects of a brand—primarily the colors, fonts and logo associated with a brand. It can be tempting to focus on that aspect of marketing when creating an online presence. However, branding is about so much more than just visual design. In fact, the visuals of a brand are typically the last part of the brand creation process. Prior to developing our brand visually, we need to develop our brand voice. It's the voice of our brand that informs the creation of the visuals, and I'm so excited to take you through this process.

Before we dive in, let's first articulate what a brand is and what a brand does.

Branding has everything to do with perception. A brand tells a story, evokes certain feelings and emotions, and generates certain expectations. Ultimately, your brand is what positions you in the marketplace and differentiates you from your competition. Your brand voice literally "calls in" your ideal customers.

Branding helps our ideal clients to:

1. Differentiate us from others who offer similar services
2. Develop a connection with us (know, like and trust)
3. Remember us
4. Choose us over our competitors!

When we differentiate ourselves in the marketplace based on who we are and what our brand stands for, that differentiation will inevitably influence the way our potential customers perceive us, and when that perception is desirable, it creates positive emotions that result in attraction and connection, ultimately leading our customers to purchase from us.

This process is what I call the Branding Continuum:

Differentiation -> Perception -> Emotion -> Attraction -> Connection -> Transaction

The branding continuum describes the process that takes place when your ideal customer experiences your brand. Branding is all about creating an experience for your ideal customers: *How do they want to feel? What motivates them? What do they value?*

When your brand evokes the feelings your ideal customers desire to feel, when it motivates them to action and speaks to and connects with their values, you'll find that you'll attract an audience of buyers in no time.

YOUR BRAND ARCHETYPE

Carol S. Pearson's work on brand archetypes has been extremely helpful to me, and I have utilized the following chart, based on her work, when helping my clients to identify their brand voice and to dial into values that matter most to their audience.

As you review the chart, you will intuitively be drawn more strongly to one or two of these brand archetypes, which will help you to further understand how to position yourself in the marketplace. It will help you target the feelings and emotions you want to evoke from your audience.

BRANDING IS INTRINSICALLY TIED TO THE VALUES AND PERSONALITY OF YOUR IDEAL CUSTOMERS AND IS TYPICALLY AN EXTENSION OF YOUR OWN VALUES AND PERSONALITY BECAUSE "LIKE ATTRACTS LIKE."

Let's take a look at how this works in real life.

I want you to take a moment to think about your favorite brands. Think about clothing brands, technology brands, restaurant/food brands, jewelry brands, car brands, and personal brands. Think about why you love those brands and how they make you feel.

One of my favorite brands is BMW®. I like the idea of a sports car, but I am also into luxury. BMW® is both sporty and luxurious. I value the workmanship and the way that you can count on a BMW® to operate. It is truly what I consider "the ultimate driving machine."

Driving a BMW® makes me feel powerful and elegant. It's just very ... me.

So how did I come to feel this way about BMW®?

The way I feel about BMW® was developed first through my experience with their branding and second, through my experience in driving and owning one.

Now I get it, not everyone cares about feeling powerful and elegant. Depending on your personality and your values, you might not be jiving at all with how I feel about BMW®. And that's the whole point of branding—to appeal to your ideal audience and to make them feel what they most want to feel, while repelling all others. When you differentiate, you will attract some and repel others. This is normal and desirable. BMW® would not appeal to someone who values practicality and being understated, would it?

Branding is intrinsically tied to the values and personality of your ideal customers and is typically an extension of your own values and personality because "like attracts like."

Archetype	Motto	Values	Examples
The Creator	*If you can imagine it, you can create it.*	Invention, Ingenuity, Creativity	Apple®, Dyson®
The Caregiver	*Let me help you.*	Community, Compassion, Nurture	Campbell's®, TOMS®
Royalty	*Nothing less than the best will do. I will have what I want.*	Control, Power, Domination	Rolex®, Mercedes®
The Jester	*Life is a party!*	Fun, Enjoyment, Light-heartedness	GEICO®, Old Spice®, Poo-Pourri®
The Guy/Girl Next Door	*Everyone matters; let's be friends.*	Belonging, Humility, Friendship	Levi's®, IKEA®, Budweiser®
The Lover	*I only have eyes for you.*	Romance, Intimacy, Passion, Sensuality	Godiva®, Victoria's Secret®, Chanel®
The Hero	*Never give up, never give in. Where there's a will, there's a way.*	Courage, Boldness, Mastery	Nike®, the Marines, Tony Robbins

Archetype	Motto	Values	Examples
The Outlaw	*Rules are made to be broken.*	Rebellion, Living on the Edge, Revolution	Harley-Davidson®, Richard Branson
The Magician	*Dreams do come true.*	Belief, Transformation, Destiny	Disney®, Oprah Winfrey, TED®
The Innocent	*Keep it simple, keep it pure.*	Purity, Simplicity, Safety	Dove®, Aveeno®, Whole Foods®
The Explorer	*You only live once!*	Adventure, Pioneering, Independence	Jeep®, North Face®, Indiana Jones
The Sage	*Knowledge is everything.*	Wisdom, Education, Knowing	Harvard Business Review®, Forbes®, Google®

YOUR BRAND VALUES

So let's engage in an exercise together and identify what we value the most.

I want you to circle the top twenty words that most resonate with you when you read the following list. You might want to start by circling all the words that appeal to you and then begin to pare down from there.

Abundance	Accomplishment	Adventure
Authenticity	Beauty	Belief
Bliss	Bravery	Candidness
Capability	Charm	Cheerfulness
Class	Comfort	Confidence
Compassion	Courage	Dependability
Directness	Efficiency	Elegance
Encouragement	Excellence	Excitement
Exploration	Fairness	Faithfulness
Fitness	Freedom	Friendliness
Frugality	Generosity	Genuineness
Grace	Heroism	Honesty
Hope	Imagination	Impact
Independence	Insight	Inspiration
Intelligence	Innovation	Joy
Kindness	Knowledge	Leadership
Learning	Logic	Love
Mastery	Mellowness	Optimism
Opulence	Passion	Perceptiveness
Persistence	Playfulness	Poise
Polish	Pragmatic	Prosperous
Refinement	Practicality	Prudence
Serenity	Smartness	Spiritedness
Stability	Thoroughness	Thoughtfulness
Uniqueness	Wisdom	Wittiness

Great job! Now I want you to pare down the list—to the top ten. I know this is difficult, but it will help you to identify your values and therefore, your voice. And of course, there might be other words, not included in the chart above, that you could choose.

When you pare down, think specifically about your brand archetype and what your ideal customers want to feel. You might have circled a word that describes you personally but might not necessarily be used to describe your brand.

For example, I would describe myself as adventurous, but I don't incorporate that aspect of who I am into my brand. My brand archetype is Royal/Magician. My ideal customers are not necessarily seeking adventure, primarily. They are seeking excellence, transformation, and divine wisdom. They want power and control over their lives and value those things more than adventure. If my brand archetype was Explorer, adventure would be a must-have.

YOUR BRAND VOICE PERSONALITY PILLARS

Let's take it one step further and pare your list down to the top five values and create adjectives from those values that describe your personality. So if one of your top values was authenticity, you would describe your voice as "authentic." If one was *dependability*, your voice personality pillar would be "dependable." These five personality pillars will shape the tone of your brand voice. Allow these five personality pillars to guide you in everything you say and write.

_____

_____

_____

_____

_____

YOUR BRAND BELIEF STATEMENT

Finally, I'd like for you to craft your brand belief statement. You see, when it comes to purchasing, people do not just purchase what you offer, they purchase why you're offering it. So as a writer, you can think about it this way: People will not just purchase your book because of what it's about, they will purchase it because of why you wrote it and how it affects them.

For instance, if you were writing about finances, you would need to be aware that financial books are a dime-a-dozen. Why would anyone purchase yours? They'll purchase your book on finance based on what you believe about finances and what it means for them. Crafting a message about what you believe about your area of expertise and being able to articulate it well, will draw your people to you. What is the deeper mission and the bigger "why" as it relates to your audience?

Below is an example from my own business. I focus on helping Christian women market and sell their products, programs and services.

> I believe that God is working powerfully through entrepreneurship and that He's raising women into places of influence and income in the marketplace to change lives, legacies and generations for His glory—and any time a woman steps more fully into her entrepreneurial calling, the Kingdom is expanded.

This is why I do what I do! This is why I help women excel in business. It's all about the call on their lives and the Kingdom impact that my ideal clients are created to make. Now it's your turn. Take some time to craft your brand belief statement and write it down. You can use this statement for social media posts, for videos, interviews, and speaking events.

By this point, you should have identified your brand archetype, your brand values, your personality pillars and crafted a brand belief statement. Way to go!

Finally, I want to encourage you to be fully you as you show up and speak to your audience. I had a coach once say, "The only one who can be masterful at being you, is you!" And it's so true! God's created you so uniquely, and the more you embrace your unique voice and story, the more you'll resonate with those you're meant to serve.

And here's the truth, there are people God's assigned to you and who will only hear what they need to hear from you, and no one else. There is literally no competition when it comes to those God has appointed and anointed you to serve. They will know you by your voice. So speak loudly from the core of who you are, and your tribe will find you.

You can find out more about Anita Albert-Watson at www.yourkingdomcalling.com.

25

ENJOY YOUR SELLING PROCESS

STRINGS OF MELTED MOZZARELLA stretched from the lasagna to my fork. But I put it down again without taking a bite. I'd been enjoying conversation with a friend in the small Italian café, but one sentence had made me lose my appetite.

"Nika, I'm telling you the truth. I assumed you wanted me to be honest with you," he said, dipping bread into a saucer of oregano-infused olive oil. The warm fragrance that had been so inviting just moments ago, now turned my stomach. "You are entering a new season and advancing to a new level. You need to know the truth. Books are a business."

I'd invited a family friend to dinner because I'd finally decided to self-publish my memoir, *Twelve Clean Pages*. This gentleman had had a vibrant career in Christian publishing, and was a meaningful influence in my life, always cheering me on. My hope for the night was that I would receive a blessing and prayer as I moved forward with my writing career in a significant way. I had certainly received that, but I had also received a glimpse behind the secret curtain of publishing, and I wasn't prepared for the raw facts I found there.

When I had told him about my decision to self-publish, he had asked me about my plan to sell the books. The question felt abrupt. Selling the books? I had not considered it at all. My focus had been exclusively on publishing.

I stammered through an answer. "Well, I … when people hear me speak at conferences they will buy books … I think. Also, I will … um … tell people about it … and people will find me online … and word of mouth, maybe?"

"You don't have a plan to sell your books? Is that what you're telling me?"

"Um … not really. The whole … selling thing hasn't been … um, finalized, yet."

"Okay. How many books do you hope will sell?"

"I … well, I think I can sell … a lot."

"How many is a lot?"

I had no idea how many. The only numbers I'd ever heard any authors talk about were astronomical. So those figures had to be possible, right? Surely, they were possible. Phrases like "more than a million copies sold" and "New York Times bestseller" came to the forefront of my mind. Those were the only gauges I'd ever heard anyone use. The flat look on my friend's face made me second-guess repeating them out loud.

I straightened my back and chose a random number, hoping to redeem myself and sound more credible. "I would love to sell 500,000 copies," I said with new-found confidence. Half a million books sold. Not too ambitious.

My friend, well-seasoned by a lifelong career in the publishing industry, looked at me, compassion in his eyes. Then, he loved me enough to take aim and fire. An under researched goal like that is rabid and has to be put out of its misery.

"Nika, I'm going to tell you the truth. The average author sells far fewer books than you realize. If you are one of the lucky ones, you will sell about 1,500 copies."

And that's when I lost my appetite.

Oh, how much I have changed after two decades in the industry.

Not long ago, I was listening to a podcast episode that featured a Christian writer for a guest interview. She had self-published several of her previous titles, and the podcast host asked her if she were planning to self-publish her next project.

"Yes," she said. "In fact, I just finished a novel a few days ago, and I plan to self-publish it next week."

"You are going to surprise your readers? Don't you want to warm them up to the idea of buying your next book?" the host asked.

"Oh, I don't care if anyone ever buys it. I just wrote it for the fun of it."

My mouth dropped. Had she just said that out loud?

Dear writer, let me tell you what I wish I could have told her: It is not noble to not care about selling your book. It doesn't make you superior that you have decided to write an entire manuscript "just for fun." It makes you unwise.

A doctor doesn't say, "I don't care if anyone ever gets well; I went through four years of medical school and a year of residency just for fun."

A construction foreman doesn't say, "I don't care if a family ever lives in this house; I have been managing this project in the hot sun just for fun."

A preacher doesn't say, "I don't care if anyone ever gives their life to Jesus; I studied the Bible and read commentaries and crafted this sermon just for fun."

An attorney doesn't say, "I don't care if this criminal ever lands behind bars; I created an argument based on the evidence in this case just for fun."

A teacher doesn't say, "I don't care if my students ever graduate; I designed this lesson plan to meet state education standards just for fun."

If you don't expect a financial return from your recreation, then what you are doing is a hobby. But if you don't expect a financial return from your occupation, then what you are doing is a *jobby*.

Hobbies require some time, some money, and some effort for *some* return.

But jobbies require much time, much money, and much effort for *some* return.

No, thank you.

Life is too short to have a jobby. You can and should be experiencing much return from much investment. In order to have much return, you must learn how to sell.

If you just threw up in your mouth a little, then pay close attention. My perspective on buying and selling could significantly shift your life. In fact, you might save money, get out of debt, lose weight, declutter your home, or look for a new occupation after you read this chapter. There's a strong possibility that nothing will look the same to you.

Let's begin with a simple quiz:

1. Which answer most closely describes your general opinion of a salesperson?
   A. *Someone who is thinking of you.*
   B. *Someone who is thinking of themselves.*

2. Which answer most closely describes your general experience the last time you were listening to a salesperson present a pitch while you were looking for a car, enrolling for a service over the phone, or talking at the front door?
   A. *Ahhh! I felt hopeful and refreshed at the end of our chat.*
   B. *Uggh! I couldn't hang up, shut the door, or get out of there fast enough.*

3. Which answer most closely describes your general feeling after your last purchase from a salesperson?
   A. *This product/service is amazing! I'm so glad I made this decision.*
   B. *This product/service is junk! Why did I fall for the sales pitch?*

Let me guess: Your answers were heavy on the Bs. No wonder you cringe at the idea of selling.

1. WHAT MOST AUTHORS THINK—Public opinion is the first reason most authors don't reach the level of book sales they have dreamed about and deserve. They don't want others to think less of them. When almost everyone you know describes salespeople with words like dishonest, unethical, fast-talking, pushy, insincere, slimy, or sleazy, then you tend to shy away from the idea of selling.

2. WHAT MOST READERS NEED—The second reason that most authors don't reach the book sales they have dreamed about and deserve is because they never overtly tell people to buy their books. In every social media post, speech, or email, they neglect the **CTA**. A CTA is a Call-to-Action, or the invitation to your readers to begin a transaction, whether paid or free.

The one thing CTAs have in common is the next step. You must tell your readers exactly what you want them to do. The average human being is low on gumption, and we won't go after things we aren't sure of. Half the time, we won't even go after things we *are* sure of unless someone suggests it to us and snaps us out of distraction. (Think, "Would you like fries with that?") If you are not offering, that's why they aren't buying.

I wish I could emphasize the following sentence by painting it in six-foot, neon green letters on a billboard: YOUR BOOK SALES ARE ALWAYS UP TO YOU.

3. WHAT MOST AUTHORS DON'T BELIEVE—See that "neon green, billboard sentence" I just wrote right there? That would be the third reason that most authors don't reach the book sales they have dreamed about and deserve.

They don't believe the billboard.

I have been coaching new writers for a long time now, and they all think (hope, pray, wish) that the secret to author success is that traditional publishers will handle all of the marketing and sales on their behalf. Some writers won't even consider self-publishing their book because they "don't want to have to sell it." And the reason they don't want to have to sell it, is because they are uncomfortable with money. Actually, let's get specific. They're uncomfortable talking about it, having it, and asking for it, but they certainly don't mind dreaming about it. Unfortunately, dreaming about money is all you will ever do if you do not learn how to be comfortable with talking about it, having it, and asking for it.

But money doesn't have to be uncomfortable because it's only a piece of paper that represents the value you assign to something. And value is not absolute. Not everyone assigns the same value to the same things.

Case in point: I don't really like anything made of crystal. It just doesn't appeal to me.

Once I saw a crystal glass with a filigree gold rim that was valued at more than $500, or so says the Internet. But I do not agree with that valuation and wouldn't pay it. In fact, if I had seen that glass for a buck fifty in a thrift store, I would have walked right by it. On purpose. I don't even care what high-end brand was stamped on the bottom.

Why? Because I am not a value match with crystal. I don't want it.

But if I were to see brightly colored, vintage floral dishware in the same thrift store? Well, baby, now you're talking! I would happily pay top dollar for a few place settings.

I am a value match with vintage floral dishware. I want it.

Selling is nothing more than agreeing on a stated value and making a match. When there is a value match, there can be a transaction or trade.

A value match happens when both the buyer and the seller believe that what the seller has to offer is more valuable than what the buyer currently has. That is clean selling. The seller wants the buyer to come out on top. It feels good when we are sold in that way because the seller is serving us.

A value mismatch happens when both the buyer and the seller do not believe that what the seller has to offer is more valuable than what the buyer currently has. That is slimy selling. The seller wants to be the one who comes out on top. It feels creepy when we are sold in that way.

A VALUE MATCH HAPPENS WHEN BOTH THE BUYER AND THE SELLER BELIEVE THAT WHAT THE SELLER HAS TO OFFER IS MORE VALUABLE THAN WHAT THE BUYER CURRENTLY HAS.

THIS IS CLEAN SELLING: I offer my private coaching package at a premium investment, and I do this because I know that my clients see amazing outcomes in a brief amount of time by using the tools I teach them. They make back their investment and more. I know the individualized attention and the results they create will bring a tremendous return over the course of their lives. I truly believe my coaching is more valuable to them than the money they have right now. When a potential client believes the same thing, we easily agree, and not because the money is easy for them to come by. It is because their assigned value in me, in personalized coaching, and in themselves is so high that what happens next is miraculous: They guarantee their own success.

The buying decision is entirely theirs from beginning to end. I am just there to tell them what I have to offer. If they do not think that what I have to offer (wisdom, mentorship, and guidance) is more valuable than what they have (money, time, and effort), then we don't agree, and they absolutely shouldn't buy from me. We are not a value match, and it is best that we part ways with smiles on our faces and a peaceful, easy feeling in our souls.

THIS IS SLIMY SELLING: A good coach knows when and where to be transparent so they can help others avoid the pitfalls they have experienced

Sigh. Here we go.

Years ago, I didn't understand selling. Neither my books nor my coaching were making enough money for me to live on. Of course, consultation calls were tense for me. The moment a potential client started second-guessing the value of their ability to create results, I would get nervous. I knew they were about to walk away because they thought what they had (time, money, and effort) was more valuable than what I had (wisdom, mentorship, and guidance). And here's the problem: I thought the same thing. I needed to pay my bills so badly that their money felt like the most valuable thing in the transaction, not my coaching. But I still tried to convince them that my coaching was the most valuable thing. I didn't realize it, but I wasn't telling the truth about what I really believed. Something feels off for a buyer when a seller tries to convince them to purchase. The thing that is off is belief. You can't fake belief. Genuine belief always shines through. If the seller does not believe that what they have to offer is more valuable than what the buyer currently has, then it doesn't feel right to the buyer. They can sense they are being taken advantage of. They run, and they should.

In those early days, many potential clients decided not to work with me, and they made the right decision. From the first moment on the consultation call, I was not in the place to truly serve them at the highest level. The seller should never try to come out on top.

MONEY WAS MADE FOR THE KINGDOM, AND IT BOWS TO THE KING.

If selling your book is hard for you, your thoughts about money probably need an upgrade.

Money was made for the Kingdom, and it bows to the King. There is a tremendous amount of godly work to be done around the globe, and in order to get it done, we need money in the hands of the good guys. When more Christians understand that, we will be able to supply critical provision for unmet needs in our neighborhoods and nations. But too many followers of Jesus assume that He considers it honorable to scrape from paycheck to paycheck.

So the very people who have been taught to share have nothing to share.

Let me say it again for the people in the back.

The very people who have been taught to share have nothing to share.

When did God say this was what He wanted?

When did the One who made diamonds and gold and silk and pearls decide that we should stay away from nice things?

I don't see it in Scripture. What I see is that God wants money to be in its proper place in our hearts, whether we have a little or a lot. Both poverty and wealth are magnifiers. Poverty magnifies what we already believe, as does wealth. The rich person can think about money too much and the poor person can think about money too much. Both are in the wrong. Both have lost sight of their Provider.

I used to look at examples of people I knew who lost their meaningful relationships, left the church, and destroyed their families when they gained substantial wealth. In an effort to protect myself from their fate, I became leery of generating a lot of income.

But now I understand that the money didn't make the mess. The person did. Wealth revealed the unfaithfulness that was already there.

What a surprise it was when the stronghold of my false belief broke! Suddenly I could see evidence that I'd been blind to before. Right now, I could tell you about several impoverished Christians I know who have lived terrible and wicked lives, crushing the people around them and forsaking the Lord. Not having money did not automatically make them good. Poverty revealed the unfaithfulness that was already there.

The other side of the revelation is that now my eyes also have been opened to the handful of life-long friends, both my parents' age and my own, who are multi-millionaires. They are prayerful, loving, humble, attentive to needs, and have been true to their families and faith the whole time. It's almost like I had forgotten all about them. I guess when I thought money was a bad pursuit for a Christian, I had only been evaluating one piece of evidence: those who hadn't handled it well.

Here is an important exercise for anyone who senses they may need a fresh perspective on money. It is a twist on an assignment from the book *Emotionally Healthy Spirituality* by Pete Scazzero (10 out of 10, highly recommend). Take time to consider your family's Ten Commandments of Money. What were the spoken and unspoken understandings about wealth? By exploring your memories, you may laugh (or cry) that you have had a false belief your whole life.

One of my family's commandments was that we were never to drink anything but water at a restaurant. Never, ever. No one was to mention it. The topic of beverages better not come up when the waiter comes around. After I left home for college, the first time I ordered a soda with my burger, I felt like I needed to call my mom to ask for forgiveness.

I'm kidding.

A little.

The wild thing that happens when we take a look at our long-held beliefs about money is that the blindfold starts falling off. I'd bet most of the commandments on your family's list are nice but not necessary.

How do I know they aren't necessary? Because there is a real Ten Commandments of Money. God would never give us something as powerful as prosperity without an instruction manual, and those instructions are found in Exodus 20 (paraphrased, obviously):

1. YOU SHALL NOT PUT MONEY BEFORE ME.
2. YOU SHALL NOT MAKE MONEY INTO AN IDOL.
3. YOU SHALL NOT MISUSE MY NAME TO GET MONEY.
4. YOU SHALL REMEMBER THE SABBATH DAY WITH YOUR MONEY.
5. YOU SHALL HONOR YOUR FATHER AND MOTHER WITH YOUR MONEY.
6. YOU SHALL NOT MURDER FOR MONEY.
7. YOU SHALL NOT COMMIT ADULTERY WITH MONEY (DON'T PUT IT BEFORE YOUR SPOUSE!).
8. YOU SHALL NOT STEAL MONEY.
9. YOU SHALL NOT LIE TO GET MONEY.
10. YOU SHALL NOT COVET ANYONE ELSE'S MONEY.

There you go. That is the golden standard. Everything else is a golden calf. There's no need to add to what God has said. Let the Lord give you as much wealth as He wants to give you. Go ahead, start selling your books with wild abandon.

Remember, we want money in the hands of the good guys. So first, be a good guy.

Then get money.

26

HELP YOUR MEDIA PARTNERS

by Michelle Rupp

YOUR BOOK IS WRITTEN. CONGRATULATIONS! Now, how do you get publicity and let the world know about your outstanding masterpiece?

I spent 20 years in broadcast news. Television to be exact. I worked as a morning show producer and, later, as a general assignment reporter. At the end of my career, I was the main evening anchor. Now I lead a communications, public relations, and business promotion boutique that increases the visibility of small businesses and nonprofits so they can increase their revenue.

The strategies I share in this chapter will enhance your opportunity of standing out and landing media coverage. We are living in a time when it is easy to rely on social media as our primary method of "getting the word out." But it is not the only way. With a little bit of elbow grease, you can create opportunities to promote your book in your local news. Please do not overlook the eager audience of people who would offer word-of-mouth recommendations, simply because they saw you on TV, heard about you on the radio, or read about you in the paper.

A computer or phone screen is not your only option.

In public relations, there is a phrase: "earned media" or "earned content." Both refer to publicity that is not paid for by advertising. It is coverage you earn; it is organic for your brand.

One of the first steps in generating this free publicity is to create a **press release**. A press release is a one-pager that hits the highlights of your book and includes a couple of memorable quotes from the author.

It begins with a dynamic lead sentence, centered on the page in a large font, bolded. Directly beneath the lead sentence, there is a secondary sentence in italics and bold. These two sentences need to answer the *who, what, when, where, why,* and *how* questions that comprise relevant news. This allows the journalist to craft the story based on the information you provide.

Your press release should include the name and phone number of the media contact, which could be yourself or someone representing you. It should also include where the book is available for sale—online, in a bookstore, or both—and a **boilerplate** at the very bottom. A boilerplate is a summation of you as the author. The boilerplate can include how long you've been writing, how many books you've written, and where you are originally from. It is no more than five sentences. There are plenty of press release templates online that can guide you in its creation.

Once a press release is complete, it's time to distribute. Distributing a release means emailing it to all the television, radio, and newspapers in your area. Check the stations' websites for their *Contact Us* section. In the case of television, that link should lead you to a *news tip* or *newsroom* email address. Radio and newspaper websites generally offer addresses with similar names. Whatever email address comes up is the one to use for distributing your release.

If you cannot find an email address, reach out the old fashion way by picking up the phone, calling the station, and asking for the appropriate person to receive a press release. Be sure to mention if there is a particular morning, midday, noon, or early afternoon show on which you'd like to be featured. In that case, you should ask for the name and email address of the specific producer of that show.

A good rule of thumb is to send a press release two to three weeks ahead of an event, such as a book reading or signing. The week of the event, send a **media advisory**, which is a quick recap of the upcoming event that includes details—dates, times, and locations—as well as notice about whether the author will be available for interviews. Media advisories go to the same email address as the press release.

MEDIA DEFINITELY WILL NOT COME IF THEY DO NOT KNOW.

It is a good public relations practice to ask the venue or bookstore where you are hosting the event if media would be permitted to attend. Assuming the owner or manager says yes, be sure to state in the media advisory that media is welcome at this event. This is most helpful, as the store is a private business, and media is not allowed to walk in with cameras without permission.

If you have received a favorable reply to your press release and media advisory—and even if you have not heard back, yet—following up with a phone call to the newsroom never hurts, especially on the day of the event. Remember, news changes in an instant. Journalists and photojournalists rarely promise coverage, but if they have the opening in the news day, they will be eager to cover a good story like yours.

Always keep this in mind: Media definitely will not come if they do not know.

If any part of this process feels overwhelming to you, there are businesses and individuals who will write and distribute press releases and media advisories on your behalf. Lack of personal experience and expertise should never be a barrier to the exposure of your amazing book.

You've worked so hard to write and publish it. Now it is time to promote!

The art of getting onto a show to promote your book is called **pitching**. Pinpoint the station and specific show on which you'd like to be featured. If there are multiple TV stations in your area, why not go for all of them?

Here are a few dos and don'ts when it comes to timing your pitch:

DO pitch around a holiday and offer to be a guest on the holiday itself. News happens 365. Shows and newscasts still go on, even on Christmas Day.

DON'T pitch the week of Election Day. It will never be seen.

DO pitch an angle that is interesting and unique. If you are pitching a book about boat safety in the summer, offer the use of your boat for the story.

DON'T pitch a story right after a catastrophe. Events that involve violence in a public place, hurricanes, tornados, winter storms, or the death of a prominent figure will always take precedence over the launch of a new book.

You want to pitch to the producer or executive producer. This will involve a little legwork, as those names and email addresses are almost never available on a station's website. Again, pick up the phone, make a call to the newsroom, and ask for the name of the executive producer (EP for short). Depending on station size, some employ this position, some do not. If not, then ask for the name of the producer of the specific show. The information you want is a name and email address. All it takes is a 30-second conversation, and you will have what you need.

Just ask.

On rare occasions, the person who answers the phone in the newsroom might give you the appropriate name and then transfer you directly to that person. If that happens, be ready to pitch on the spot! You can pitch over voicemail, but be concise and leave a phone number. Add that you will follow up with an email and then do it.

When pitching via email, make the subject line and the first sentence memorable. This is a must. Producers and EPs can field hundreds of emails in one day. Why make the subject and first line memorable? Everyone gets email on their phones so that first line needs to grab them too as they are deciding in an instant to click it or keep scrolling. You may consider typing the word **{PITCH}** in brackets before the dynamic subject line.

THE INTERVIEW IS THE AUDIENCE'S CHANCE TO GET TO KNOW YOU.

Once you've successfully pitched and are booked for the show, or if a reporter (also known as "the talent" or "the personality") has agreed to interview you, it is up to you to make your moment in the spotlight as effective as possible. Here is how to further help the producer and talent create a memorable promotional opportunity for you:

PROVIDE TALKING POINTS.
Talking points are questions. Provide five. The last question should always be, "Is there anything else you would like to add?" This gives you the opportunity to mention a website or event during the feature. The other questions must be informative about the book, and personal about you, its author. Where are you from? How did you start writing? How has your life changed since fulfilling the dream of becoming an author? What prepared you to write on this topic?

You want to know the questions the talent is going to ask in advance, and providing talking points will put you at ease. It minimizes the risk of having any curve balls thrown your way. You will be able to speak concisely and communicate effectively, and it will lower your stress levels. Trust me, the morning of the interview, you will have plenty of time to get stressed about being on TV. At least you will already know the questions and answers.

BE PERSONABLE.
The interview is the audience's chance to get to know you. Create that connection. Do not come on the show and just sell. Keep the viewer in mind. The host will lead you down the road and give you a natural opportunity to offer ways the public can find you. Look at the talent who is speaking to you, not toward the camera. You are having a conversation with the on-air personality; the cameras are merely there to eavesdrop on that conversation. And most importantly, don't forget to smile.

MAKE IT VISUAL.
Television is a visual medium. The audience wants to see something, not hear it. What visuals can you offer as you promote your book? Are there illustrations? Provide those ahead of time to the producer, not the morning of. Did your publisher offer to create YouTube videos of your book? Provide a 30-second clip to the producer. Did you do a book reading, signing, and take video on your phone? Provide that video of audience members listening as you read or shaking your hand as you sign their book. Get creative and do everything you can to make the interview visual.

Include visual elements in the pitch by mentioning what you have for them to use in the feature. Add a sentence or two that you will provide illustrations or a 30-second video clip or video from your most recent signing. The more preliminary work you can do for the producer, the better your chances are of being featured on the show. If you provide talking points and visuals in advance, you've basically done the work for them. Also offer to provide a book, understanding they may or may not take you up on it. As a former producer, I genuinely appreciated guests who provided content and made their appearance beneficial to the viewer. Often they were invited back!

WEAR CLOTHES THAT MAKE YOU FEEL CONFIDENT.
Bright colors are always the best practice. If you are someone who doesn't embrace color, you

can never go wrong with neutrals: black, gray, navy, burgundy, or olive green. Skirts, dresses, and slacks are all a personal choice for females. For males, select a dress shirt and tie. However, if it is the middle of summer and 100 degrees, a three-button shirt and khakis is appropriate.

Ask yourself this question: Would you wear the outfit to a job interview? If the answer is yes, then it is fine for television. If the answer is no, head back to the closet. Your television feature is the ultimate job interview, held in front of a large audience who is considering whether to say yes to your book. Make their choice as easy as possible.

A valuable piece of advice is to stay away from prints. They look great in person, however some prints come alive on camera and almost shimmer or "buzz." Houndstooth is a great example of this. The problem is, you never know which print might come alive on camera until it happens. It's a distraction you do not want. The viewers will be too busy looking at your jacket, skirt, or tie, and will not hear a word you say! It's best to avoid all prints for this reason. You want the focus on your book, not your clothing.

PRACTICE.
Your time on TV will be short. It will feel like it's over before it starts. If you are an in-studio guest, you will have between two to four minutes. That's it. If you are being interviewed at a bookstore, the reporter will ask you a lot of questions. However, the final piece that runs on the evening news might only include one sound byte from the interview. That's why you must practice. Practice your responses. Work on polishing the answers. When the bright lights and little red camera light come on, cortisol can shoot through the roof. The more you practice, the more it becomes a habit and the less likely you are to forget important points you want to make when you hear, "We're back in 3 - 2 - 1 ..."

Finally, a few days after your appearance, do something thoughtful for the show producer. Your grandmother was right: Never underestimate the importance of a thank you note. But

I challenge you to take it up a notch and consider having cookies delivered to the station as your thank you. Don't make it extravagant; you would never want to appear to trade food for a segment. However, sending cookies, cupcakes, pastries, or donuts to a morning show is a memorable touch. Include a brief note of thanks, and you are golden. The next time you come with a pitch, you will be remembered in a flattering way.

When it comes to pitching a radio show or local newspaper, most of the same rules apply. Obviously, there will not be cameras, visuals are not essential, and the reporter will have more than just a few seconds to fill, therefore the interview will be lengthier. Still, providing talking points ahead of time is helpful. Newspaper reporters are more likely to want a copy of your book and will create their own questions after reading.

With so many online entertainment and media choices available, we have access to the world. However, there is still something unique about local news, print, and broadcast. It is still a viable avenue for exposure. When you can help your media partners by providing convenience, then the ability to create earned media opportunities makes the positive publicity that much sweeter!

You can find out more about Michelle Rupp at www.memorableresultsmedia.com.

27

SERVE YOUR PEOPLE

by Myron Golden

YOU CAN BECOME TRULY GREAT. Even if your book isn't very good, you can become a great author when you understand the Kingdom of God and your place in it.

What is the Kingdom of God?

The word *kingdom* is a compound word from the word *king* and the word *dominion*. So the Kingdom of God is the King's dominion—the dominion over which God is King. The Kingdom of God is God's magnificent obsession. When God created heaven and earth, He created earth as an expansion of His heavenly Kingdom, a physical realm over which He could rule.

First, He created Creation: The sun, moon, stars, trees, water, etc.

Next, He created Creatures: dogs, cats, alligators, creeping things, fish, birds, etc.

Finally, He created Creators: man—an extension of Himself to rule over the expansion for Himself. Man is a God-like creative with flesh and blood. God made man to dominate the earth.

That is where we must begin. It is important to have this Kingdom perspective when reading the teachings of Jesus.

In Mark 9:1, Jesus said to His disciples, "There be some of [you] that stand here, which shall not taste of death, till [you] have seen the kingdom of God come with power" (KJV). The next thing He did was take Peter, James, and John to the Mount of Transfiguration, where He glowed like a light and met with Moses and Elijah. They all had a mountaintop experience, and immediately after they came down the mountain, the disciples met a man who had a son who was possessed by a devil. The man asked the disciples to cast out the devil, and they couldn't do it. So they came to Jesus, and He cast out the devil.

Then He turned to them and said, "The Son of man is delivered into the hands of men, and they shall kill him; and after that he is killed, he shall rise the third day."

The disciples didn't know what He meant.

This could have been a teaching and learning moment for them. The disciples could have asked Him what He meant. But they were afraid to ask.

> IF YOU WANT TO KNOW SOMETHING THAT GOD KNOWS, DON'T BE SCARED TO ASK HIM. FATHERS LIKE IT WHEN THEIR CHILDREN COME AND ASK THEM THINGS.

Can I recommend something to you? If you want to know something that God knows, don't be scared to ask Him. Fathers like it when their children come and ask them things. What reason is there to be scared when He said, "If ye then, being evil, know how to give good gifts unto your children, how much more shall your Father which is in heaven give good things to them that ask him" (Matthew 7:11 KJV)? So if you want to know something, just ask. Who better to ask than the One who created everything?

But in the case of the disciples, instead of asking Him what He meant, they got into an argument with each other. Isn't that so much like us? When we don't understand something, we get into an argument about it, thinking, *Well, if I don't understand something, at least I can pretend I understand.*

The passage goes on to show us that Jesus noticed them arguing, and when they arrived in Capernaum, He asked them, "What was it that ye disputed among yourselves by the way?" He wasn't asking them why they disputed because He didn't know. He was asking them because He wanted them to say it.

The disciples didn't answer Him, because "they had disputed among themselves, who should be the greatest."

They were saying:

"I'm the greatest!"

"No, *I'm* the greatest!"

"I'm the one that went up on the mountain with Him!"

"I'm the one that suggested we build a ..."

"I know, but I heard Him, and He said no when you told Him you wanted to!"

"Don't y'all know He called us *The Sons of Thunder*? I *know* we're the greatest!"

I can hear the argument right now. It's so interesting that we human beings want to be acknowledged by other human beings for being the greatest.

And Jesus heard what they were arguing about. How do we know? Because they had "held their peace" and never answered His question about their dispute. Yet, He sat down with them and said, "If any man desire to be first, the same shall be last of all, and servant of all."

I'm going to give you the master key to greatness. Are you ready?

Look for people to serve.

In fact, serve everybody. And realize that if you serve people what you want to serve them, you are not really serving them. You are using them to serve yourself. Serving people is not serving them what you want to serve them. It's serving them what they want to be served.

We have to serve the *people*. Really poor servers at a restaurant serve food. Great servers serve *people* the food. Really horrible teachers teach a subject. Great teachers teach a *student* a subject. We don't serve things to people. We serve the *people*. In fact, we have to learn to love serving the people.

God put you here by yourself but not for yourself, and He put me here by myself but not for myself. I would be a miserable excuse for a human being, if I were just looking for people to serve me. I would be miserable because I would never be able to find people who do it well enough, and I would always feel unfulfilled.

But if I am looking for people that I can serve, I will never feel unfulfilled.

Do you know how you can serve every human being you come into contact with? It's free, and everybody can do it: smile.

When you smile, you will get a reflection back to you of what you are.

And what about an encouraging word?

Let's say you feel love and appreciation for someone in your heart. You feel it, but you don't actually say it or show it. Then you did not serve them.

When Jesus said, "be last of all," He was saying we should put other people's needs for encouragement or a smile or resources above our own needs. Stop going around, looking for people to be an answer for you, and start looking for people that you can be an answer for.

STOP GOING AROUND, LOOKING FOR PEOPLE TO BE AN ANSWER FOR YOU, AND START LOOKING FOR PEOPLE THAT YOU CAN BE AN ANSWER FOR.

Jesus said if you want to be the greatest, you need to be the "servant of all." Who is *all*? All includes the person at the airport that you just walked past and didn't look at because you were too busy to say hello and acknowledge the Godlikeness in another human being. Your encouraging word and your smile might be the thing that keeps them from jumping off a bridge that day.

Or you go to a store, and someone gives you an attitude so you give them an attitude back because you think it's about you. What if instead, you said, "It looks like you are having a bad day. I want you to know that I care, and I am going to be praying for you?"

We have to serve the people God puts in our path. Walking in the Spirit means to listen *for* what the Spirit says and then listen *to* what the Spirit says.

That was the point Jesus was making to the disciples. Because the next, He took a child into His arms, and said, "Whosoever shall receive one of such children in my name, receiveth me: and whosoever shall receive me, receiveth not me, but him that sent me."

Why did He take a little child?

When He is showing you how to be the greatest, why would He use a child as an example?

He was saying that your greatness is not measured by what you do for the people who can pay you back. He said your greatness is measured by the people you serve who have nothing to offer you. That's why when I am with people, I watch how they treat little children and senior citizens. I watch how they serve people.

Do you want to be great?

You may never be great in the eyes of man for putting yourself last and being a servant, but you will be great in the eyes of God. We have to look at the people we come into contact with and decide that we will treat them well because that is what we are called to.

I believe that the Kingdom that God desires to set up on the earth will solve all social problems—all the social problems in your family, all the social problems in your business, all the social problems in government, all the social problems in schools, all the social problems in universities. It will solve all the social problems everywhere if we just apply the principles of the Kingdom of God.

What are those principles?

PRINCIPLE 1: I yield my life to God as the Sovereign King. I realize that He's running things, and I am not. So I'm not going to treat you the way I want to treat you; I'm going to treat you the way He wants me to treat you. I'm not going to talk to you the way I want to talk to you; I'm going to talk to you the way He wants me to talk to you. I'm not going to engage with you the way I want to engage with you; I'm going to engage with you the way He wants me to engage with you.

Guess what happens when I yield my life to God as the Sovereign King? He gives me an assignment to rule over. And when God gives us an assignment to rule over, we are the only human being in the history of the world who can fulfill that assignment.

PRINCIPLE 2: I use the assignment God gave me to rule over to serve every human being I come into contact with. Then I am the greatest. I am the greatest Myron Golden that God created me to be. I'm yielded to Him, ruling over my assignment, and I am serving people. You become the greatest *you* when you are doing the same thing. Most people resist yielding to God, they want to rule over someone else's assignment, and they want to use other people to serve them. It's the exact opposite of what God put us here for.

If everyone started vying to serve instead of to be served, it would change the game forever. If you want to compete in your business, compete to see who can serve the most. If you have a desire to serve people, a desire to make people smile, a desire to encourage people, and you have a desire to operate in business from a place of excellence, then everything changes. You may not even be the person who is the best in your niche, but if you will adopt the motto, "Nobody is going to serve with greater intent than I am," people will break the door down and climb over the walls to do business with you.

But you can't come into a marketplace, seeking to get as much as you can from that marketplace and think you are going to be successful. You might be successful for a little while, but you'll never be successful long-term unless you show up and shine for the purpose of serving.

What if every time you met another person, you were looking to see what you could give instead of what you could get? How would that change the world?

We can see a biblical example of what it would look like to have that kind of service mindset in the life of King Solomon.

In 1 Kings 3:5 and following, we read, "In Gibeon the Lord appeared to Solomon in a dream by night, and God said, 'Ask what I shall give thee'" (KJV)?

Solomon responded, "And now, O Lord my God, thou hast made thy servant king instead of David my father: and I am but a little child: I know not how to go out or come in."

What's he saying? He's saying the assignment God gave him to do is bigger than him. He's saying the job God gave him to do was something he didn't know how to do. He knew he was insufficient for the task. All of us have felt that way at some point.

The conversation continues:

> "And thy servant is in the midst of thy people which thou hast chosen, a great people, that cannot be numbered nor counted for multitude. Give therefore thy servant an understanding heart to judge thy people, that I may discern between good and bad: for who is able to judge this thy so great a people?"
>
> And the speech pleased the Lord, that Solomon had asked this thing.
>
> And God said unto him, "Because thou hast asked this thing, and hast not asked *for thyself* long life; neither hast asked riches *for thyself,* nor hast asked the life of thine enemies; but hast asked *for thyself* understanding to discern judgment; behold, I have done according to thy words: lo, I have given thee a wise and an understanding heart; so that there was none like thee before thee, neither after thee shall any arise like unto thee. And I have also given thee that which thou hast not asked, both riches, and honour: so that there shall not be any among the kings like unto thee all thy days" (emphasis mine).

Why does Solomon ask God for "understanding to discern judgment?" Because that was the king's job. He was asking God to give him the wisdom to do the thing that God put him here to do in a way that pleased God and served the people God put him here to serve.

Wouldn't that be a great prayer for all of us, all day every day?

What if every father and mother woke up and prayed, "Dear Lord, give me the wisdom today to be the father or mother You put me here to be and serve these children You put me here to serve?"

What if every husband woke up and prayed, "Dear Lord, give me the wisdom today to be the husband You put me here to be and serve this wife You put me here to serve?"

What if every wife woke up and prayed, "Dear Lord, give me the wisdom today to be the wife You put me here to be and serve this husband You put me here to serve?"

What if every employer woke up and prayed, "Dear Lord, give me the wisdom today to run this business in a way that pleases You, and also serves these employees You put me here to serve?"

What if every employee woke up and prayed, "Dear Lord, give me the wisdom today to be the best employee I can be in a way that pleases You, and also serves this company You put me here to serve?"

What if every politician and pastor—what if every human being—prayed that prayer every day? What if that was our whole heart's desire?

I'll tell you what would happen. Every time you created a product for the marketplace, it would be the best product possible, and people would be banging your door down to buy it.

This is how you can become great, even if you are not that good at what you do. See, all of the stuff you are looking for in your entire life can be found in becoming the greatest servant of all.

AS LONG AS I AM YIELDED TO GOD, MY ASSIGNMENT HAS TO YIELD TO ME.

Yield your life to God as the Sovereign King of your life and rule over your assignment. When I am ruling over my assignment, I'm not wondering if it will work. I know it has to work. As long as I am yielded to God, my assignment has to yield to me. It doesn't have a choice. I don't have to try hard to do it. I just do what I was put here to do. It's going to work. Why? Because it's under me. How do I know it's under me? He put it under me. I'm under Him, and it's under me. I don't have to worry about it not working. I can work on it as if there's no chance of failure, as long as I'm yielded to Him.

Isn't it interesting that God installed in us the desire to serve people with what we create, with how we connect, and with what we contribute? Those are the things that make us feel fulfilled.

When I meet another human being, if I can create a solution to their problem, I will get paid. I have to stop thinking about my problem long enough to focus on someone else's problem. One of the reasons entrepreneurs struggle is because they are trying to use the marketplace to solve their financial problems. But if you fix the problem that the marketplace knows it has, that will fix the financial problem that you know you have. You don't have to worry about yourself. You can put yourself last, and you will be first.

You might be saying:

"But I don't have a degree!"

Good. Go serve.

"But nobody knows who I am! I only have three followers on Instagram!"

Good. Go serve. Is your Instagram to serve other people, or is it to serve you?

"But nobody watches my videos!"

Good. Go serve. Maybe the stuff you're saying is what you're interested in, instead of what they're interested in.

"But I wrote a book, and it's not selling!"

Good. Go serve. Maybe you should write a book that the marketplace wants to read, instead of writing a book that you want to write.

The answer to every problem in your life is this:

Find somebody to serve.

You can find out more about Myron Golden at www.myrongolden.com.

The following is an excerpt from:

TWELVE CLEAN PAGES

a memoir

THE SIRENS WERE SINGING MY NAME. I could hear them coming for me, calling to me, crying out as the ambulance spun around the street corner. Another moment might have been too late. Tires ground to a halt at the curb, and the mournful whine died. Red beams flashed into the bedroom.

Two paramedics barreled through the front door, and my mother ran to them. I started vomiting. Lying on my back, I could not raise or turn my head to spit the refuse out. I could not open my mouth. Trying not to inhale, I waited in agony.

This is it. Right now. This is the end. Right here.
At twenty years old.

After resting a gurney near my feet, the EMTs dropped on their haunches; one knelt close to my face. His words were long and wide with a Texas accent, and he talked to my mother over his shoulder casually, as he assessed my motionless body. I wanted him to move faster. The other paramedic mentioned, in polite tones, our freshly painted front door. They had pushed into the bright red stain as they fell inside.

"Y'all should have put up a Wet Paint sign," he said amicably. It sounded as if he were showing the scarlet smear on his forearm to her, chatting as if he had come to call on a family friend.

"Oh," she said, noticing.

The paramedics knew what they were doing. As long as they could distract my mother, she would not be looking at me. They were trying to prevent her from descending into panic while they rescued her only daughter, a task they were not sure they could do.

I screamed inside, *Pay attention to me! Look in my mouth! Look in my mouth! I am about to choke!*

When I started heaving again, vomit erupted from my nose and forced my lips apart. They all quieted suddenly, and the EMT nearest me quickened his pace, turning my jaw, scooping tongue and throat with gloved fingers. Both men lifted me onto the gurney, and we were out the door and into the ambulance in one brilliant motion. One of the men instructed my mother to drive her minivan when she tried to climb in beside me.

"You're gonna need to follow behind us, ma'am."

She rushed off, and the paramedic jumped up after the gurney, carefully maneuvering in the cramped space.

"I want her with us ...," I said with labored breath.

"It's not like the movies, kid," he said, warning me. "This is going to be a rough ride, but I've got ya." The back doors slammed, and he squeezed in at my side.

"I heard ya hate needles," Texas said, chuckling. His kind voice smiled down on me. "Then the last thing you want is for me to stick ya while we're in this racing vehicle of mine. So let's make ourselves a deal, huh? You stay awake for me, and I won't stick ya. Lemme hear you talkin'. C'mon now."

"Hold my hand," I whispered.

"Atta girl." The ambulance lurched forward, and he clasped my hand in both of his, holding tighter as we gained speed. "Here we go."

Our street was luminous in the night as the fire engine, ambulance, and minivan pulled away from the house. My seventeen-year-old brother, Mark, sped into the neighborhood just then and whipped his steering wheel around to join the swift convoy on the tail end. When the emergency vehicles entered the near lane on the main road, the fire engine broke away from the corps, and the ambulance quickly took the lead with lights only.

Mark had not expected this. He knew I was getting worse, knew I needed to get to the hospital immediately, but when he turned onto our street and found it blazing like a carnival fairway, his spine stiffened. Employing a last-ditch logic, he convinced himself that it was not a life-or-death situation until they fired up sirens along with the lights. He willed himself not to feel fear.

I could not hear the screaming traffic because my right ear was ringing at an alarming volume. It was both a high-pitched squeal and a low buzz. My senses were dulling; there were only the paramedic's voice, my thoughts, and the awful noise in my ears.

Tex took away his hand when I became very still. We were two minutes into the ride. "Stay with me, kid. I don't want to have to stick ya. Talk to me. Talk to me." He rapped his knuckle on my sternum.

"Hold ... my ... hand."

"That's it! Stay awake. Keep talkin'. As long as you talk, I can hold your hand. No more fadin' out on me. Got it?"

My eyes had not opened since my mother had made the 911 call. The hospital was twenty minutes away, in downtown Fort Worth, and the longer we drove, the more peaceful I became. A soothing sensation eased through me. I melted into a consciousness of one solitary breath at a time. Concentrating, I took another. And, carefully ... another.

"I told ya to stay with me!" He knuckle-knocked my chest again. It was a hard jolt, jerking me from the warmth into which I had been sliding. Now the buzz seemed to sizzle out of my right ear and down my entire right side, burning my arm and leg. Nerves crackled under the skin. A fiery hum lit each joint. There was a distinct line down the center of my body. On the left side, I felt normal. On the right, aflame.

"You gotta keep talkin' to me!"

Everything I had been thinking and wondering slowed. All thoughts coalesced into a liquid unit of information, like a swelling drop of water on a rainy window ledge.

Just a singular sentence in my head: *This is what it feels like to die.*

No life-flashing-before-my-eyes experience. Just emptiness. No wishes or promises or bartering away. Just serenity. The paramedic had been right. This was not like the movies. I knew I was dying, and I was not afraid. Only the essential continued to occupy my thoughts.

A second bubble of information: *I want someone to hold my hand.*

"Hold ... my—"

"There ya go! Wake up, now!" As I came to the surface, I realized that he had been shouting at me. He pounded my sternum with greater strength now. "Stay with me! C'mon, kid! C'mon!" He struck my chest until his voice cracked, and I heard him choke with feeling.

Suddenly he stopped.

The back of the ambulance was still, hushed. He leaned close to me. Warm breath faintly brushed my cheeks. I could tell he was looking directly into my eyes, as if my eyelids would flutter open by the sheer force of his will.

We sped along in silence, face to face.

Then he whispered, "Can you see them, kid?" Compassion rose in his voice. It was a final, quiet plea. "Look. Can you see their faces? Look at them."

I took a slow and shallow breath.

"Look. Can you see them? Those are the people who haven't had a chance to love you yet. Please, don't take ..." He paused.

I inhaled.

Regaining his voice, he said, "Don't take their chance away, kid. Look at their faces. Don't take their chance away."

Exhale.

Then, like breaking clouds, my austere thought pattern parted, and I could see face after smiling face in my mind. None were faces I recognized. I wanted to tell him. I wanted to tell him that I could see their faces, but I made no sound.

The ambulance tore into the emergency drive, and my new friend expertly released the bed, throwing open the back door simultaneously.

"We're here, kid," he said.

The last drop of thought fell: *Thank you.*

My brother finally allowed himself to be afraid in the hospital elevator. He and our mother had had to hurry to catch up with the men who were running the gurney down the hallway. They all crammed in closely beside me for the claustrophobic ride up to the ICU. Breathless, Mark watched the paramedic snap his fingers repeatedly in front of my face. In a fevered attempt to rouse me, the EMT was leaning over, talking loudly, and urging me to stay awake. Mark could sense our mother's desperation as she stood vulnerable and voiceless at his arm.

I do not remember anything about shuttling into the hospital or taking the elevator or entering the ICU in a blistering rush.

By then I had lost consciousness.

You can purchase your copy of Twelve Clean Pages *at any online retailer.*

For the Kingdom.

www.ingramcontent.com/pod-product-compliance
Lightning Source LLC
Chambersburg PA
CBHW080036120526
44589CB00037B/2664